The Unofficial Family Archivist:

A Guide to Creating and Maintaining Family Papers, Photographs, and Memorabilia

Melissa Mannon

Library of Congress Cataloging-in-Publication Data
Mannon, Melissa
Preserving Memories: Maintaining Personal Papers, Family Photographs, and Memorabilia / Melissa Mannon.

     p. cm.

 Includes bibliographical references and index.

ISBN-13: 978-0-9827-27614

1. Archives—Administration. 2. Public history—United States.

Cover photo collage by Melissa Mannon. Image upper left—tintype of doctor, author's collection. Image upper right—the author's mother, Montreal, Canada. French correspondence—author's collection.

www.archivesinfo.com

Dedication

To my daughter Lorelei, my nieces Miriam, Rebecca, and Julia, and all the generations that will follow us. May our family stories forever remain a vital part of our communities.

Table of Contents

Acknowledgments

This book would not have come to fruition without the enthusiastic support of the many people who have attended my "Preserving Memories" and "Life in Context" workshops. Your welcoming attitude helped me get over a fear of public speaking so that it has now become one of the most enjoyable parts of what I do. Thank you for twenty years of attentive listening, contributing, and sharing of your family stories.

Special thanks to my "Life in Context" partner and friend, Sue West. Her support for everything I do has helped motivate me and has aided my personal and business growth over the past couple of years. Sue's gentle constructive criticism was indispensable on a few difficult chapters in this manuscript.

Thank you also to Erica Holthausen, whose enthusiasm for everything is infectious and sustaining.

Appreciation also goes out to Christine Destrempes and Nancy Schrock for reviewing parts of this manuscript.

I would also like to acknowledge my mother. Her family stories helped shape who I am. I am extremely grateful that she has always shared the good and bad tales that showed me a path toward becoming a better person.

Finally, I want to give another special thank you to my editor, Jennifer Zumpano. Knowing that I will have a gifted critical eye to review my work in the end makes this whole process much easier.

Introduction   *The Unofficial Family Archivist*

Introduction

The Role of This Book

Fourteen years ago, my husband and I bought and moved into our first house as a couple. I began unpacking personal papers and heirlooms that had been boxed in apartments for years. They would have taken up too much space in cramped quarters for me to permit their release from confinement, but our new home afforded us the room to settle in and unpack the things that represented our family memories. As I worked, I took time out to flip through long-neglected albums and began noticing problems with them. All of the causes for concern were common preservation issues I confront every day as an archivist: The images of my childhood in the 1970s were beginning to discolor. The glue on the "magnetic" pages on which the pictures were stuck, not intending to budge, was browning. I found that I needed my professional skills in my personal life. Up until that time, I primarily thought of applying my archives background to collections within institutions. After this experience, I began thinking of all archives (records with long-term value) and personal memorabilia within anyone's possession as mini "collections," requiring similar care to those materials housed in professional repositories.

> *"Within every home is a treasure trove of information."*

Within every home is a treasure trove of information. Unfortunately, many irreplaceable documents that help tell individual stories, and the stories of our communities, are deteriorating among our personal belongings. Photographs are turning yellow and fading. Papers are growing brittle. Staples holding items together are rusting. Files are getting lost among growing digital trails. The documents and keepsakes we have gathered over the course of our lives are often not given the attention they need to maintain their physical condition. Few are given organizational structure or are labeled in a way that would be understandable to people who do not have a direct connection to the items. Many memories are getting lost in piles of personal "stuff." In my work as an archivist and consultant for the last eighteen years, I have found that most people think that their family records are important, but they do not know how to properly maintain them.

This book focuses on the care of personal papers, photographs, and memorabilia. Personal papers are created by individuals and families and are one type of archives. Archives are the recorded information that we create in any form during the course of our daily activities. They document our lives and shed light on our personalities, actions, and values. They tell about how we function in society. They include information about our communities and the culture that surrounds us. Our photographs help illustrate these moments. In addition to creating this information during our lifetimes, we also collect "memorabilia" that is meaningful to us and helps describe our activities. Memorabilia makes it easier to celebrate the events and special occasions we cherish. Ribbons picked up at state fairs, postcards from trips, and buttons we wore in support of campaigns tell much about who we are and what we value.

Clients often tell me that they have been called or see themselves as "the family historian." They develop an interest in family history that is sometimes sparked by finding old papers or photos in their home, or they are thrust into the role when they inherit a pile of old materials. Interested in the past and concerned about the neglect of the resources that shed light on it, the family historian attempts to care for these materials with little guidance. This book will give you or the person protecting personal papers the knowledge needed to begin caring for materials thoughtfully and in a competent manner. You will be capable of creating a valuable resource that you can access for family information and will learn how to safeguard your materials for the future.

The Unofficial Family Archivist: A Guide to Creating and Maintaining Family Papers, Photographs, and Memorabilia grew from a presentation focused on one aspect of safeguarding personal materials—the act of preserving them. I have addressed varied audiences on this topic in a workshop I offer titled *Preserving Memories: Maintaining Family Photographs, Personal Papers, and Memorabilia*. I find that attendees are often people with an immediate need. They bring in treasured personal papers and objects that they see are in danger. The materials are usually discolored, disintegrating, or moldy; items are brought in shoeboxes and manila envelopes. Simple changes in the way they are kept will promote their longevity, but there are other aspects to consider. This book addresses a wide variety of topics so that you gain a broad, encompassing perspective on your personal items and the history they represent.

Think of the papers in your home as a "collection." This grouping of materials tells the story of your life. People who influence you, important events, and topics in which you take interest should all be represented. The papers you create are the raw information (or the "primary sources") that one would use to write your biography or examine to better understand how you lived and worked among your peers. Think about how your personal papers represent you. What aspirations and activities are evident that explain the real you? How do you want your children to remember you? What personal papers among your archives show your humanity and highlight your role in society? When we save the records of our past and work to define the context for them, we strengthen our family traditions and values. We increase our knowledge of humanity and better our communities. Understanding a personal and larger history goes hand in hand with protecting its resources.

The Unofficial Family Archivist is organized into eight sections that discuss preservation and other methods you can use that will protect your family history. Topics relate to creating and identifying materials that represent you; how to properly organize, preserve, and describe these items; and how to prepare them to pass on to future generations. This book provides information to guide you so you may enjoy your materials, easily access them, feel comfortable that they will last for a long time, and be confident that you can pass them on to future generations.

Important Things to Keep in Mind as You Read

First, please realize that it is not necessary to be perfect. For example, my home has wide temperature fluctuations from one end to the next. Though changes in temperature increase the possibility of materials disintegrating, I do not have much choice. Most of my materials are stored in the room that is hottest in the summer. This is not ideal, but that is where they fit, so I make do. Rather than focusing on achieving all of the suggestions in this book, focus on those that you can most easily achieve first and work to improve things over time. Do not get frustrated if you cannot afford all of the supplies that I recommend, do not have perfect storage conditions, need to keep certain things separated throughout your house for space reasons, or cannot identify all of the people in your photos. Changing just a few things about the way you care for your personal papers can greatly increase their longevity and informational value.

Second, consider your personal papers as a whole. Take account of your old and new records. Think of all the materials that represent your life. The concern that you have for the letters your mom passed on to you should be given the same care as the emails you send to your daughter in college. "Personal papers" can take a variety of forms. The information that we collect and create is becoming more complex over time, but the basic strategy for viewing your materials as a whole "collection" representing you remains the same. The basic archival methods described here—preservation, arrangement, description—apply on a general level regardless of the medium of your personal papers.

The Unofficial Family Archivist: A Guide to Creating and Maintaining Family Papers, Photographs, and Memorabilia explains the basics of managing personal papers in a way that is understandable to nonarchivists, while retaining accuracy about archival methods. Some of the information is quite in-depth for those who wish to fully control their personal papers. The chapters on arrangement and description primarily are those that go into more detail than many users may want or require. Adapt and abridge the field standards for your individual needs and do not see them as a set prescriptive to which you must adhere.

This book highlights a selection of the personal collections for which I have cared that are held by small repositories in New England. These samples demonstrate how individuals and families living their "normal" lives can prove extraordinary to future generations. Some of these stories make up the most respected parts of the American psyche from major events such as the Gold Rush, the Civil War, and the suffrage movement. They include the struggle of immigrants and working professionals. They reveal common people with big dreams that often take them to great places. They should serve as models for caring for your own materials and demonstrate the value of each life story to a larger history. In the appendix, I outline these and other collections from repositories with which I have no professional affiliation that are also mentioned in the book.

The end of each chapter includes short exercises to help you with the care of your family records. A glossary at the end of the book may clarify unfamiliar words. Though I would like to avoid jargon, I think it is important for readers to get a handle on the most common words that archivists use when they think about collections and caring for cultural heritage resources. The words are intended to inform and to spur interest. I do not want them to be a source of frustration. The technical names for things do not matter—the concepts behind them do.

The Chapters

Family heritage keepers need to consider whether they are passing on a well-rounded collection of experiences through their written pieces of lifetime evidence or whether they are just passing on bits that leave more questions than answers. The first chapters of this book explore how to ensure that you are keeping the important things. I teach you how to eliminate clutter to highlight important resources. Removing unimportant papers from your files tightens your remaining items into a core collection of valuable informational resources for your family. Chapter One helps you begin thinking about the important elements and stories of your life. Chapter Two assists you in identifying which records best reflect your narrative to help you form a strong informational source.

Then, whether preparing your records for your own personal use or for future generations of relatives or community, this book assists you in making your family information accessible. After reading this book, you will be able to put in place an organizational system for family papers that highlights your life and values. Chapters Three and Four introduce established arrangement systems and accepted, easy techniques for preparing collection indices or lists of documentation. They explain how recording the subject matter found among your materials and creating an inventory of file names provides additional assurance that your organized collections are also comprehensible. For those interested in more thorough tools for "indexing" collections and ways to make information more accessible, I introduce a few professional concepts for describing collections. Among these are describing the scope of the collection, including essential biographical information related to the creator(s) of the materials, and other elements that provide a more complete overview of one's personal papers.

These chapters are particularly important because many people have told me that they are concerned that family materials are not valued, and that once they no longer personally care for them, the items may be discarded. This book will eliminate anxiety concerning the future security of your family's history. The value one can inject into a family collection through proper boxing and description methods makes the need to properly maintain the materials obvious to anyone who takes over archiving responsibilities after you. Your preparations will secure materials as a noteworthy family asset.

In Chapter Five, we explore preservation problems and techniques that keep items safe to ensure their longevity. This section explains the basic elements that cause deterioration so that you can avoid common problems. I provide information about storage supplies and what to look for in a safe storage space. I make you aware of issues for which you should seek expert help and where to get that help, while providing tricks for smaller pesky problems, such as eliminating a musty smell from materials. My goal is to show you that a few simple measures can make a tremendous difference. I offer advice about disaster preparedness to ensure that you are ready in the face of a threat such as a flood.

Chapter Six encourages you to also think about what aspects of your life are not recorded. We explore projects for recording previously undocumented information. Oral history, journaling, crafting, and more are considered and examined for appropriateness in documenting personal history. Readers are encouraged to try to capture a sense of place in their written records. I explain how different formats are valuable for conveying different information and also to suit different personality types.

Chapter Seven discusses digital information. Thinking about electronic documents as a standard part of modern personal archives, I describe their unique preservation and management needs and explore how to deal with common personal digital files. I note places where we leave our digital footprint, how to organize our electronic personal information, the role this information plays in telling a life story, and the challenges ahead for maintaining information in a quickly changing digital environment.

The final chapter of this book encourages individuals to consider donating materials to local repositories to add pieces to a puzzle of a community history. The addition of personal papers to established collections helps ensure the protection of a larger cultural heritage. This chapter discusses how to approach local professionals to donate papers, how to provide information about your family's historical role in the community, and what to consider when offering your papers to an institution.

Cultural Heritage Collaborators

This book relates to the concepts presented in my previous book, *Cultural Heritage Collaborators: A Manual for Community Documentation*, which aimed to encourage partnerships among cultural heritage repositories and communities. *The Unofficial Family Archivist* further explains the role of families to ensure the complete documentation of historic events in our times. These two books may be used together to encourage communities to take better care of their historical resources.

I promote the idea that, beyond their family connection, our personal papers tell what it is, or what it was, like to live in a particular place at a particular time. Within cultural heritage institutions around the world are the personal papers—diaries, correspondence, photographs, and other documentation—of common citizens like you and me. Our stories are important for understanding what it means to be of a certain race, sex, or ethnicity. All of our historical documents, whether kept in professional repositories or in private homes, have value to the human story. We must all work together to make sure our heritage is secure and that the documentation that tells this story is inclusive and comprehensive.

This book unlocks the world of professional archivists so that you are aware of how your personal materials relate to those held by cultural heritage repositories. It introduces you to archivists' methods and how to get in touch with an archivist when you need additional assistance. It provides information about fields related to archives management, such as museum studies and library science. Our personal papers are a valuable resource that forms the backbone of history, but materials hidden in homes and unknown to cultural heritage experts often hold as much historical value as materials found in professional repositories. I encourage you to seek partnerships with professionals who can help you better understand your personal and community history. I encourage you to play a part in working with professionals to create a plan for effectively documenting your community and your contributions to your community.

Use this book to start thinking about your collection and your place in history. Treasure your personal papers and recognize that they are a valuable cultural asset. You can choose to highlight your place in civilization through the records' care or inhibit your legacy with their neglect. Recognize that the role you play as an individual can assist cultural heritage institutions formed with the purpose of preserving wide-ranging heritage. Your role as an "unofficial archivist" is vital for capturing personal experiences that illuminate larger trends. By maintaining your papers and supporting the care and safekeeping of diverse historical resources, you help guarantee the long-term memory of civilization. Know from where we came so that we can better plan where we are going.

Chapter One:
Your Story

Why Save and Preserve Your Story

- Self-discovery—define yourself, create a clear vision of your life
- Instill personal pride
- Work out personal problems
- Organize thoughts
- Remind yourself where you've been to figure out where you are going
- Notice how you change; notice personal growth
- Pass on memories
- Record significant family events, genetic issues, cherished stories, and traditions
- Teach and pass on what you value—morals, beliefs, ideas
- Record your views on time and place for community
- See yourself in a larger context as part of a bigger story

From "Life in Context Workshop" by Melissa Mannon and Sue West (www.lifeincontext.org)

Personal Narrative

A narrative is a series of descriptions about connected events that form a story. Your personal narrative is the account of your life that includes details providing a well-rounded view of your personality and existence. This book focuses on archives as the foundation for your own personal tale. I aim to show you which documents reveal your individual narrative to reflect your unique and valuable personal history.

In this chapter, we begin to consider what your documents say about you. We later determine which items are most important to your family story. I encourage you to view your personal papers as a collection and see if they can be used to weave together an adequate picture of your life. Do they show your personal point of view? Do they effectively tell what is important to you? Do they show how you function from day-to-day? Do they show how you relate to the world around you?

Think of yourself as the center of history. How does a telling of your actions relate to a larger tale of society? Your materials reflect your life as a representative of the modern world. Your story is one of a number of similar stories about people living in your town, or with your occupation, or with your hobbies. Many things about you are paralleled by others with similar interests, backgrounds, and lifestyle. Your papers help tell your own personal narrative but also reveal a larger narrative of our society. Your documents reflect who you are—by caring for them with intention, you have the opportunity to help mold your legacy. Throughout this book, keep in mind that your work as an unofficial family archivist helps ensure that your personal narrative is an adequate accounting of who you are, how you have grown, your role in the world, and how you have influenced others during your lifetime.

There is much value in considering your personal narrative. An examination of your life story can help you create a clear vision of where your life is, how you got here, and where you are heading. It can help you establish an identity rooted in heritage that can evoke personal pride. Understanding your life story makes it easier to pass on your memories to your loved ones. It helps you record significant family events, genetic issues, and heirloom stories that will be valuable to future generations. It enables you to teach and pass on what you value in terms of your morals, beliefs, and ideas. Considering your personal history enables you to record your views of time and place for your community. It helps you generate compassion and empathy as you place yourself in context as part of a larger community. Discover new things about yourself and your connection to

Our Personal Narrative in a Public Arena

My mother recently reminded me of how personal some seemingly impersonal official records are when we talked about how her dad had served in the American military as a displaced Polish citizen after World War II. My grandfather assisted with post-war cleanup efforts and, despite not yet being an American citizen, he was officially discharged from the United States Army when his work was done. This is likely the first official tie of any sort that my mother's family had to the country to which she would move to when she was just a little girl. This piece of paper was created by the government for administrative purposes, but it also represents all that my grandparents went through to escape the Holocaust in the 1930s and all of their future dreams of a new place that would accept them and where they could raise a family. Mom's collection of family documents includes records related to Grandpa's military service.

See Your Things as Part of Your Narrative

We have the power to make connections from our own lives to our communities using our objects as symbols. Notice connections between you, your things, and your community members. Why do you do the things you do? Why do you have the things you have? What are the connections?

For example, my mother owns carnival glass dishes with a view of the Brooklyn Bridge passed down to her from her mother. I collect carnival glass, in part because of my mom's dishes and the warm memories I have of her serving pretzels and dip in them. Make sure what you collect and keep has meaning. I can collect carnival glass because it is beautiful or I can connect it to something more important in my life.

Using the objects in our life as launching points for our narrative can make the storytelling easier.

others by giving a little thought to your role in this world.

We automatically know some of the items that are reflective of our life story. Certain documents are valued as objects of pride and for the warm remembrances they provide. These materials evoke memories of moments and life passages we treasure. We can easily relate to these materials with deep personal meaning as part of our narrative. We want people to see the best of us and are sure to incorporate these materials into our life story. For example, I want to remember my days as a successful high school athlete as reflected in my awards and sports scrapbook. I also want to cherish my diplomas. And, my photographs of my wedding will always be on prominent display in my home.

However, reflecting on a legacy should also involve the seemingly mundane or the rough patches of our lives. A truly reflective personal narrative better preserves our memories, mixes good and bad, and reveals our humanness. The good things that have happened in my life make me happy. The ways I deal with the less-than-perfect things are part of my learning process and are as much a part of me as the best bits. I want to remember these things so I can see how far I have come and so I can appreciate the good even more. I want my daughter to understand what I went through in my lifetime so she can learn from my experiences and make her own life even better. Difficult times in my life— including getting bullied in junior high school, searching for a job for more than a year after grad school, being unable to get pregnant when I wanted to, and having had breast cancer—are stories worth sharing along with the happy ones.

Your personal story was not created by you alone. You are influenced by others, and you have the capacity to influence others as well. The more elements you identify in your narrative, the more communities you can weave into your life story. Identify your connections to the outside world.[1] Your knowledge of these connections can be a powerful tool to help you better understand yourself and the world around you.

We may locate bits of our story among the papers of family members. We also can look a little further. Public documents show how we function within a community, showing our connections to various institutions and individuals while placing us within a context of contemporary events during a particular time and place. Individuals are not the only ones who can and should treasure personal narratives. Communities and institutions should take note of the stories that define their existence. We must remember and value the idea that individual narratives come together to form a larger shared history.

Detailing a Life

Breaking down the elements of a life helps you understand the things that are important for evaluating your personal history. I am creating a detailed outline of "Home Life" here as one example.

Home Life

- Family members
- Neighbors and townspeople
- Day-to-day activities (getting up, drinking coffee, emptying the dishwasher, etc.)
- The physical house and landscape (what it looks like, how it has changed over time)
- Special recurring events (holidays, differing activities with seasonal changes)
- Notable events (a move, a house fire, a wedding in the yard, visitors)

---

[1] The story at the end of this chapter, written by Diana Whitney, shows a woman trying to figure out her communities, how they relate to her life story, and how they reflect her view of herself. It is interesting to see her working to redefine her role in the world. "Am I Jewish?," *Washington Post,* August 30, 2010, newsweek.washingtonpost.com/onfaith/guestvoices/2010/08/am_i_jewish.html (July 27, 2011). Also see Diana's blog (www.spiltmilkvt.com).

Trying to Identify with Another's Narrative

Coca-Cola is one company that recognizes the value of personal narrative to boost its company image and appreciation for its products. We think of Coca-Cola as a great American company, in part because of the personal narrative it has developed based on its archives. The company's campaigns often focus on nostalgia. Partaking in the famous soft drink can bring back good memories of times past. Coca-Cola often dives into its archives to show us images shedding light on its own narrative, connecting it to our own. For example, remember those warm fuzzies Santa brought you as a kid, and your warm feelings of holidays with your own children? Does the Coca-Cola Santa remind you of those good times? Coke brings him back again and again to keep those amiable emotions going strong. Companies such as Disney, Hershey, and Timex continually delve into their company archives to reemphasize their narrative and add to it, continually connecting their narratives to your recollections.

Personal narratives are all around us. They are not just in our homes and our cultural institutions. We see them in advertisements trying to evoke a sense of nostalgia to make us buy a product. We see them as decoration in the form of photos and artwork of the local landscape and of individuals in community businesses. Here they mark a sense of pride and make a statement that this business is part of an established community.

We see narratives in brochures and pamphlets that invite us to become tourists and encourage us to visit a particular place that is claiming its heritage as part of its charm. Individuals would do well to look for the stories all around them and become aware of how they play on our heartstrings and how we fit them into our personal narratives. In addition to the products you use, think about the professional teams you support, the religious institutions to which you give allegiance, the civic organizations that seem to have been there forever, and the local mom-and-pop shops you frequent. Be aware that their tales can be an enriching part of life and help create strong bonds among family and communities.[2]

I remember sitting in my

---

[2] Doris Kearns Goodwin's autobiographical book, *Wait Til Next Year* (New York: Touchstone, 1997), ties the author's childhood narrative to that of the Brooklyn Dodgers. It is a good example of a tie between a personal narrative and a company one.

friend's basement and playing Pac-Man. The thought of video games, and specifically the Atari gaming system, reminds me of my childhood. I remember getting pizza every week at a local mom-and-pop shop. Baskin-Robbins clown ice cream cones were a childhood favorite and then again played a vital role in my life when I was pregnant. These and other memories of products help me form my personal narrative.

The idea of community narrative supports a strong argument to care for your personal papers. You hold stories in your head; you transfer some to record. You have the power to evaluate the chronicle of your life, understand its value, and encourage proper documentation to be created and tied to your legacy. Your story can influence what others think about you, but it can also influence what they think about themselves and others.

Finding your "voice" to describe your role in the world is part of the legacy you can leave to your children and to future generations. Your accumulated knowledge has value to those who will come after you. The best way to ensure that what you know gets passed on is to document your story. How you live is a piece of a larger tale that we must not forget. The more "legacies" we can preserve, the better we understand the narrative of humanity, allowing us to better ourselves and the world around us, preserving our freedoms, fighting against repression, opening us to new ideas, and/or binding us in our shared experiences.

You Are Always a Member of Some Community

A community is a formal or informal group with a common history. Your memories are part of a larger community memory.

Communities come in the form of:

- Families
- Ethnic groups
- Civic organizations
- Governments
- Informal and formal social groups
- Educational institutions
- Colleagues
- Causes
- Geographical locations/ neighborhoods

Your communities play a role in your makeup. You help influence your community as well. Your ideas, values, etc., help mold your personal environment.

Weddings as a Community Microcosm

My brother was married last summer, and looking around the event, I realized what a microcosm of humanity I had before me. The wedding ceremony itself—its wording and the traditions we included—tells a lot about my brother, his wife, and their communities. The wedding party's style of dress, the table centerpieces, and the food all provided clues about the communities of the people we were celebrating. Wedding attendees were all members of at least one community of the bride and groom. They were family members, or they went to school with them, or they sat and drank beers with them on Friday nights. Some at the wedding were colleagues or neighbors; others were involved in formal social groups in which the couple took part. Some lived far away; others could scooter to the ceremony. There were people with different political beliefs and different religions. Most were attached by a number of community connections.

Understanding Communities

Every individual participates in communities, either intentionally or unintentionally, through ethnicity, living space, workplaces, beliefs, and behaviors. A community is a formal or informal group with a common history or culture. The community may be based around a geographic area, trait, or topic of interest. It can be represented by civic organizations, governments, informal social groups, educational institutions, causes, and the like. Communities can also be historical. For example, if you are a dancer, Fred Astaire is part of your historical community. Your memories are part of a larger community memory. Your personal history and personal growth parallel community history and growth; your actions and stories influence the development of communities as they influence you.

All of this is reflected in your personal papers. Our written documents help us understand the groups to which we belong, how these groups intersect with others, and the similarities and differences among people. Examining communities helps us define ourselves and the world around us.[3]

Our personal papers reflect

---

[3] For more on communities in the world of archives, see "Archives and Community," *ArchivesInfo*, Sept. 27, 2010, archivesinfo.blogspot.com/2010/09/archives-and-community.html (July 27, 2011).

greater human connections and changes. They reveal a lot about an individual, including the time and place in which one lives. They also reveal much about human nature, what we have in common, and how we change our perspectives (and thus our communities) over time.

Our personal papers provide a first-person accounting of events. When we save materials with a little thought, we help provide high-quality evidence of the time in which we live. The information we keep in our homes is often the most accurate account we have of the ways people live in our society. Our records tell about us, but they also reveal our perceptions of and relationships with others. Materials within homes, when brought together, reflect diverse views that may be used to more accurately interpret our communities.

In addition to reflecting our personal narrative, these items and the personal memorabilia that we collect over our lifetimes, such as our baby shoes, are also interesting when viewed with other similar materials in different families to show trends or tastes during a particular time. Our seemingly personal materials have an alternate role as a symbol of what is important to society in a specific time and place.

Historical Communities

Every community to which you belong has a history. For example, I am a member of historical communities of women, Americans, and archivists. Each of my communities has changed over time. I would be a very different person if I lived at a different time because the expectations my communities had of me would differ. If I lived one hundred years ago, I probably would not be writing this book. I would be living in Europe. I would not be an archivist. I would clean my house and cook more often. We can see in our archives how ideas have altered. We see signs of discontent and then moves to change situations. Movements in support of better labor practices or for women's rights are part of the same historical alterations—communities rallying for a better future. Consider to which communities you belong. Take note of how your personal papers are representative of how that community functions in this particular place and time, and how that community changes through generations.

Documenting Moments

Did you know that in the nineteenth century, people often documented memories of everyday life and community connections more consciously than we do today? They more carefully recorded sales and even household purchases in special ledgers made for that purpose. Some deposited calling cards with friends when they went to visit or signed house guest books. They carefully planned gardens and recorded the seeds planted. People took photographs to document their lives. They ensured that their most prized things were included in imagery, including their homes, fanciest rooms, pets, heirlooms, and kids' favorite toys. Individuals wanted to remember the elements of their lives that were important to them so that they could hold them dear. Today, we often document haphazardly, capturing what strikes us on a whim rather than carefully considering what we want to remember.

Documenting Communities

The personal papers that we have identified and saved make up what is called the "historical record," or the "documentary record." The documentary record is the surviving written or otherwise recorded material that provides evidence or information about a society and its activities in a certain time and place. We conclude what we know of history based on the records left behind by others. Documentation helps bond communities, promoting connections among people and allowing us to evaluate society by comparing a number of sources side by side.

Many materials we will discuss in Chapter Two are not only valuable to your family—they have historical importance to your communities as well. The records in your life tell the story of what it is or was like to live in your town during a particular era. If we put together the stories of all of your neighbors, we can create a picture of a larger community—our differing beliefs, functions, family structure—that reflects the whole of our society. This is where professional cultural heritage repositories come in. Many materials that were first created by individuals much like you, and were then maintained by their families, are now treasured by archives and cultural heritage institutions all over the world.

Archives exist all around us. Individuals create them every day when they do things such as make a monetary transaction, take a family picture, sign a marriage license, or send an e-mail to a loved one. Humans leave a trail of records, some of which are immediately discarded, some that hang around forever, and some that are important for piecing together a life story or a community history. Local archivists are continually on the lookout for that last group of records—the ones that represent a community history. Such local history forms the building blocks for larger views of society.

Professionals need everyone's help to ensure that the multifaceted aspects of society are represented. In other words, we aim to ensure that we are appropriately documenting communities. Whether you are rich or poor, whether you work behind a desk or on the beam of a skyscraper, your life should be represented among our community archives. A personal diary might show how you live your life and your views of the world. Your company's business records may provide evidence about what life on top of a skyscraper is like. A simple talk about your reminiscences with a grandchild that is recorded on video to pass to the next generation can show what it was like to live through various historic events from your unique perspective.

Archivists need help finding these materials. Many of our records make it directly to the repositories we keep in town halls, government agencies, or businesses. But those institutions that focus on cultural heritage—the libraries, archives, and museums—can collect only what is given directly to them. They may try to actively seek record donors, but they often end up with materials that relate only to those who are most visible in the community or most easy to access. Your family papers, or parts of them, may have value beyond your family and may help fill gaps in the documentation that professionals can most easily come by.

Consider your personal materials alongside the American history you know. What side of the story do your personal items represent?[4]

What community narratives do your memories feed?

---

[4] Melissa Mannon, "The Citizen Archivist," *Bedford Bulletin*, July 1, 2010, www.archivesinfo.com/images/bedfordbulletincitizenarchivist.jpg (July 27, 2011).

Claiming Heritage

This story, first published in the Washington Post, *discusses the value of thoughtfully considering personal narratives and community connections. Author Diana Whitney was kind enough to let me share it.*

Am I Jewish?

Some children grow up with religion; others get a secular muddle of post-'60s consciousness. I don't pretend to be Jewish, any more than I pretend to be Protestant, or Hindu for that matter, even though I'm a yoga teacher. When people ask about my ancestry, I give them a typical East Coast melting-pot breakdown: 50% Russian Jew, 25% Swiss, 25% Irish. That 50% carries some legitimate weight, but it won't ever let me claim I'm a Jew. Jewish identity passes through the mother, and it was my father's parents who [emigrated] from Kiev.

By the time I knew them, these grandparents had retired to a snug, immaculate home in Mamaroneck, New York, crammed full of cherished possessions—a baby grand piano, an ivory-inlaid chess set. We ate Thanksgiving dinner around a polished cherry table; aunts and uncles laughed and shared jokes during the meal. No one prayed or mentioned God.

Nanny and Poppy were already old then and spoke with thick Russian accents. I was wary of them, although they were gentle and kind. Once Poppy scolded me for picking his yellow tea roses, climbing in a perfumed tangle over the fence, and I always felt shamefaced around him.

After they were dead, my father rarely spoke about his parents. He never mentioned his Jewish upbringing. Eventually I gathered that he'd gone to Hebrew school and received his Bar Mitzvah, only to have a falling-out with his narrow-minded rabbi. "A crisis of faith," he called it. At age 14 he walked out of temple and never went back again.

You can be a Jew without being a practicing Jew, of course, and my father liked to lay claim to his Jewish roots in certain situations—when justifying his hatred of the Germans, for example. He often told us he'd experienced anti-Semitism at Oxford, though not exactly what had happened. It was my mother who revived Judaism for us (albeit in American holiday style) by starting a family Hanukkah tradition. We used Poppy's tarnished brass menorah, with two ornate lions holding up the candles. My father led the Hebrew prayers in his booming baritone. I loved to hear his voice, so fluent in this strange language I stumbled over, hard consonants twisting in my mouth like nails.

I came to cherish the candle-lighting and the ritual Hebrew, the only prayers ever spoken in our house. But we passed over it quickly, eager to play dreidl for gelt and eat potato latkes with applesauce. I was proud to tell my friends we celebrated Hanukkah as well as Christmas. I wanted to be half-Jewish, to be initiated into that special club of religious knowledge. I devoured the all-of-a-kind-family series, books about an immigrant family growing up on New York's Upper East Side at the turn of the century. Through the lives of these five sisters, I learned about other Jewish holidays—Rosh Hashanah, Yom Kippur, Sukkot, Passover, Purim. But it wasn't till I took Religion I in college that I realized Hanukkah was but a minor part of the Jewish calendar.

My father once brought me to a Seder, at the home of one of his Economics colleagues. I sat next to him in confused silence for what felt like hours, embarrassed by my ignorance. Why had I never been to temple? Why did I not know a single word of Hebrew, only the Yiddish passed down from my grandmother Nanny into our jokey family culture: *shmatteh, shmuck, shmuts, toches*?

But the most shocking part of being not-Jewish came when I was 24, and my younger brother wrote a research paper for a college history class. Reading it, I discovered that my grandfather's name was not Arnold Sabot, as I'd known him, but Abraham Sabsowitz. Abe (as he was called) grew up in the Ukraine on the eve of the Russian Revolution. His father was a Talmudic scholar, and the family often went hungry—his sister Rose died from malnutrition. "I could smell potatoes growing under the ground," my grandfather remembered decades later.

At age 17, Abe joined the Green Army, a Ukrainian nationalist movement gathered to protect Jewish communities during the Bolshevik rise to power. One night, he witnessed his father shot and murdered by the Kossacks in front of the temple. My heart raced as I read the paper. How could this brutality have been inflicted on my Poppy when he was so young? How could my father have kept this secret from us? Maybe it seemed too removed from his own four children, growing up in our white- bread college town in Massachusetts. Maybe it was a tragedy my father wanted to bury forever.

The night of my great-grandfather's murder, Abe was arrested in Kiev, and his three cell-mates were executed one by one. But the jailer took pity on the 17-year-old boy, allowing him to escape. Eventually he left Russia, traveled the trans-Siberian railroad to China, then back-tracked to Kiev to rescue his mother. They made it to Poland, where Abe (a dashing fellow) worked as a traveling actor before immigrating to America. There, he got into the fur trade in Pennsylvania and became a millionaire by the age of 24. He drove a fancy Stutz Bearcat loaded down with furs and carried a pistol to protect his cargo. Then he lost his entire fortune in the Great Depression.

Despite this blow, Abe's steady faith lay in American democracy and capitalism. He believed in America with "the fervor of a convert," according to my father. Perhaps this is where the family channeled its religious impulses, for my father inherited Abe's capitalist ardor, as well as his ingenious knack of making money out of good ideas. But his Jewishness? Not so much.

As for my great-grandfather, the Talmudic scholar, murdered for his faith, no one knows his name. His grandchildren never knew it, and there are no written records. Sometimes I dream of going to the Ukraine on a romantic quest to trace my long-dead relatives. Now that my father has died as well, they seem like characters out of an epic historical novel. I also dream of going to temple here in my small Vermont town. It's not curiosity, but a deeper longing for an ancient religion that must have been transmitted to me by my ancestors. But I stay away, afraid of being branded an imposter. After all, I'm not really Jewish.

*Whitney, Diana. "Am I Jewish?," *Washington Post, *30 August 2010, newsweek.washingtonpost.com/onfaith/guestvoices/2010/08/am_i_jewish.html (27 July 2011). See her blog at www.spiltmilkvt.com/about.*

Mental and Writing Exercises for Personal Narrative

1. Write your reason(s) for recording and passing on your personal story.

2. Make a list of five of your personal items that have sentimental meaning. Why are these items important to you?

3. List three positive events in your life that changed you or helped you to grow. What did you learn from them?

4. List three personal challenges or negative things that have happened to you during your life. Did you learn anything from them? Can others learn anything from them?

5. Make a list of five things that you do every day that provide insight into your family life.

6. Make a list of products that have played a significant role in your life. What memories do you have of these items? What do these memories say about your values or your generation's values?

7. List five organizations that impact your life and play a vital role in your identity. How have these organizational "communities" changed over time? Have they changed during your lifetime? How do their community stories relate to your own personal story?

Chapter Two:
Identifying Archives

What Are Archives?

Archives by Any Other Name...

We sometimes use other words in place of the word "archives." Other terms you may see associated with archives, or types of archives, include:

- Historical records
- Historical manuscripts
- Historical documents
- Historical resources
- Primary sources
- Permanent records
- Personal papers
- Written documentation
- Institutional records
- Public records
- Vital records
- Special collections

Archives include manuscripts (one-of-a-kind written records), ledgers, diaries, photographs, original recordings including audio and visual formats (e.g., recorded tapes, records), and digital material (e.g., e-mail, archived Web sites, DVDs).

Archives are original records that we want to keep permanently because of a certain fundamental value that they possess. Personal papers are one type of archival documentation. This book focuses on these types of records, which are created by individuals during the course of everyday activities or as a result of monumental events. Personal papers provide useful historical information about a particular subject, time, or place. Or, they offer evidence of the actions of a person or group.

Think about all of the documents in your home. You have things such as your bills, your childhood report cards, and letters from your boyfriends or girlfriends. All of these materials provide information about your personal history. They show how you have lived and how you have changed. They provide information about the people close to you, as well as about acquaintances. They provide evidence that you were here—and, when considered together, these materials tell a story about your life. These are your personal papers or your archives.

Archives may include original documents on paper, photographs, digital media, sound recordings, and video recordings. Common archives include diaries, ledgers, correspondence, civil papers, legal documents, and financial records. Archives are not necessarily old. Many documents that you create today may be considered archival and worth keeping forever. Alternately, many old documents may not possess any value as archives. This chapter provides information about various types of historically valuable material, why we value it, and how we can identify it among our mounds of less important records.

Archives are cared for by professional archivists in repositories, as well as by volunteers in such institutions, and individuals in their homes. The methods discussed in this book are those employed by professionals who have specialized training with advanced degrees in archives management and appropriate hands-on experience under a more advanced professional.

Three Meanings of Archives:

1. "Archives" are records in any form that possess informational or other long-term value and should therefore be permanently retained.

    a. Archivists most officially use this term for historical materials relating to the history of an institution. When such materials are created by organizations, we tend to call them "institutional records," or just plain "archives."

    b. The term is also used as an overarching concept to incorporate the idea of any documents with long-term value. This includes "personal papers"—what we generally call historical records created by individuals. The term "archives" is sometimes used as an umbrella term to cover both personal papers and institutional records, and I employ the term in this book in that way.

2. "Archives" is also the location at which archival materials are maintained. It is sometimes also called an "Archive."

3. The "Archives" is also the organizational body that cares for archival materials, including administration, staff, and guiding policies.

Where to Find Archives

- In libraries—usually in special collections separated from the books
- In museums—containing original documents related to the museum's artifact collections
- On their own—in historical societies or special community-based archival centers
- In town halls and federal government repositories—made up of documents created by municipal and national governments
- In businesses—starting as active office files, showing daily activities of an organization, and moving to more permanent storage when no longer needed regularly
- In schools—as centers for research or repositories for records of school activities
- In homes—family papers, business records, and association files

Types of Archives

There are a number of formats for archival documents. These include the various media in which we record our experiences. Our lives can be represented by many different types of items, including handwritten papers, digital files, and multimedia (AV) recordings.

When people consider the term "records," they often first think of official documents that are vital to our identity and our possessions. Among these in our family papers are civil records related to births, deaths, marriages, and other dealings with governments. These materials may include property-related information sources such as wills and deeds. They may also include passports, military enlistments, and immigration papers. Many of these records are duplicated or exist in a separate form in town clerk offices and other government repositories.

Archives are created while we embark in diverse activities ranging from our personal lives to our businesses to our interactions with the government. Most American citizens leave a long "paper trail." Our records are not just the official kind: Information about our lives may be found within our homes and outside of them. It is a challenge to identify all of the locations where we leave bits and pieces about ourselves.

Value of Archives

One of the most important roles of archives is to serve as evidence of original thoughts and events. Where secondary source materials such as books are based on people's interpretations and are subject to misunderstandings and sometimes purposeful deception, archives are those written documents that were created as the result of an event or activity. As such, archives should be used as the primary element in research. They preserve ideas and, when collections are properly maintained, safeguard the context in which thoughts are formed and knowledge is accumulated. Scholars and others should base their ideas on the original documents they find in archival collections, combining their observations with the ideas other people have formulated and written in books and articles. When one is in doubt about something someone says, one can turn to archives for a better understanding, forming his or her own opinions based on the materials that bring us closest to the activities they reflect.[5]

Archives have the capacity to stimulate memories. We try to save the items that are most meaningful to pass from generation to generation so we can transmit

Why Save Archives?

- Preserve ideas
- Better understand culture
- Remember events
- Provide evidence
- Maintain truth
- Protect diversity
- Foster community
- Remember family
- Support understanding
- Evaluate relationships
- Sustain continuity
- Assist order
- Enhance efficiency
- Require accountability
- Ensure freedom
- Require liability
- Secure property rights
- Guide planning
- Moderate change
- Encourage enquiry
- Promote sense of place
- Document collections
- Supplement education
- Augment programming
- Define identity
- Safeguard memories

---

[5] See "Why Value Archives?" *ArchivesInfo*, 2010, archivesinfo.blogspot.com/2010/09/why-value-archives.html (July 27, 2011).

Archives Advancing Civilization

In my first job out of graduate school, I worked in a private science center, where I was charged with caring for the prized photo collection of the institution's founder. The collection was extensive and included works by well-known artists who were personal friends of the deceased scientist. When I completed my work with the images, I inquired about the man's personal papers. I was told that he kept few. He wanted his published writings to represent him and did not wish people to see his drafts or musings. The thought process leading to his final writings had not been retained for others in his field or for social researchers to examine.

What we learn as we progress can influence and further the work of others who also care about our interests. Our steps and missteps may show others a path toward success, advancing ideas and civilization. I thought the decision of this scientist was a shame and still feel that it leaves a big documentation hole in American scientific history and knowledge about our development as a society.

our knowledge to our contemporaries and to those living in the future. The common memories and shared experiences of our society inform future generations about who we are and what we have accomplished.[6]

Written records represent our recollections of the events in which we participated. They provide evidence about these events and record our impressions of life as we know it. Archives retain our history both when there is no one around to remember what happened and when it is necessary to try to objectively understand a course of events. To identify "archives," we must define the records that best represent us and the things we do. We must spot these resources among our own materials and among those of people in our communities. We must also seek diverse materials that cover a lengthy period. Such diversity allows us to understand a personal narrative from multiple angles, accurately reflecting our complexity as human beings and exhibiting a multifaceted legacy.

---

[6] Robert Archibald discusses the idea of history and shared experiences in his book *A Place to Remember: Using History to Build Community* (Walnut Creek, CA: AltaMira Press, 1999).

Archives Collections

The grouping of materials created, gathered, and saved by a person or an institution is called a "collection." A collection of personal papers has the potential to stand as a testimony to a life and to fully illustrate the story of that life. A personal collection of archives and memorabilia can illuminate the activities in which we participate and with whom. It may reveal what we think about the world around us. In general, archivists arrange materials in their care by the person or persons who created individual collections.[7] This allows one to focus on individuals and their interconnected relationships.

A group of personal papers has more value than any one lone document. Although individual documents may have value as single items, all are more informative when accompanied by other related materials. Even cherished manuscripts that we all know, such as the United States Constitution, which can stand alone as a vital piece of history, have important related information that helps us better understand their context and intent. For example, included among related Constitutional documents are the *Federalist Papers*, which provide insight about the intentions of the Founding Fathers.[8] Diverse materials in a collection help offer well-rounded views. Researchers and others can

Unusual Collections

These collections provide glimpses of unique histories. Common artifacts and historical documents are brought together to reveal uncommon stories. Think about the stories your own items help reveal.

The Asphalt Museum: http://ecs.csus.edu/~gordonv s/asphalt/asphalt.html

Kimchi Museum: www.lifeinkorea.com/Travel2 /seoul/315

Museum of Bad Art (MOBA): www.museumofbadart.org

Museum of Toilets: www.sulabhtoiletmuseum. org

See The Global Museum for links to more unusual collections: www4.wave.co.nz/~jollyroger/GM2 /unusual.htm

---

[7] The act of keeping materials together as they were found is known as maintaining "provenance." An intact group of records should not be broken up and rearranged by subject or some other artificial classification scheme. See the chapter on organization for more information.

Libraries, Archives, and Museums

Libraries, Archives, and Museums (in some circles known as the "LAM") have more in common than they have differences. Known as "Cultural Heritage" or "Memory" institutions, these organizations carry on a civilized need to preserve memories of the past. They differ in:

- Training, degrees, and standards required for professionalization
- Collection media (though materials often overlap)
- Focus on individual items versus groups of items
- Organizational and cataloging systems
- Emphasis on diverse aspects of collections, with things such as access, exhibits, programming, preservation, and documentation given different priorities
- Ways to spell "catalog(ue)"

can examine and use them to enhance understanding of context and to create well-informed inferences.

Consider your personal materials. Would someone get a good sense of the person you are from examining your wedding album? Or would he better understand you if he could see the album alongside your school reports, correspondence, and household records? The more archival records we retain about an individual life, the more clues we have about a person's history. Furthermore, the original arrangement of items can tell us a lot about the thoughts of the creator of a collection. Family historians should keep these principles in mind, working to keep records of individual family members together in a simple organizational scheme that will provide descendants with a better understanding of their personal history.[9]

A collection related to one person can be compared to those of other related individuals. Multiple collections or groups of records can provide a more accurate view of society, offering diverse viewpoints and related experiences. As mentioned earlier, it is desirable to get multiple perspectives even when thinking about one's own life. At different times, we have different opinions developing with life experience. A look at the records I kept in my teens would reveal different

---

[8] See *The Federalist Papers* from the e-text archives of Project Gutenberg and the Library of Congress at thomas.loc.gov/home/histdox/fedpapers.html.
[9] The idea of organizing your papers as a group will be explored more fully in Chapter Three.

attitudes and values than those possessed by my forty-year-old self. Similarly, materials kept by others about me would offer different insight.

The information that we have collected alongside the documents and personal archives we have created tell the story about our life journey. "The things we save give shape to our lives and reflect who we are—our interests, our values, our activities, our relationships—to our families, our communities, and to future generations. Your personal papers, memorabilia, and artifacts are part of a unique individual history." [10] Other parts of our story may be found in the homes of family members—brothers, sisters, adult children—and can be added to our materials to form a larger collection.

After considering my own personal papers, I look to my communities and consider records created by other family members. Within my home, I have materials created by and relating to my child, my parents, my grandparents, my husband, and his ancestors. These materials tell about my past, how I got where I am today, and my cultural influences. When one puts one's personal papers in the context of others, it allows one to make connections and piece together relationships. As we act within communities, we link our personal history to those of others. We may value similar things and participate in similar events, but we imprint our own point of view on what we experience. It is important to capture our unique perspective and the diversity of the perspectives among us to better document history and to place our own lives in context.

Uncovering New Chicago Archives Project

On a large scale, community documentation projects can fill great gaps in our understanding of civilization. For example, the Uncovering New Chicago Archives Project is a multi-institutional collaborative in which participants have sought documentation about the African-American experience in the city. Materials of value to the preservation of community memory were found in storage rooms, family basements, and attics. The materials are now preserved in separate collections, such as those of the Chicago Public Library and the University of Chicago.

---

[10] From introduction to presentation "A Life in Context: Telling Your Story" by Melissa Mannon and Sue West, 2010.

Your Personal History

Two years ago, I visited my daughter's class to describe what I do for a living. Adults often look at me strangely when I tell them that I am an archivist. I knew that my presentation was following a police officer and dentist and that my occupation would be much more difficult for the children to comprehend. The first-graders to whom I was speaking hardly knew what history was, so my task would be doubly complicated. I went in with a poster of Fred Astaire and Ginger Rogers, Babe Ruth, and other historical characters to whom I thought they could relate. I told them that anything they like has a history. It is my job to make sure we remember the important things that happen. I asked if Mommy and Daddy took pictures at their birthday parties. I followed by asking how they would remember and explain the party to others if Mom and Dad forgot the camera. We talked about keeping diaries, cards, and other documentation that would remind them of the event. It is important for everyone to realize that each person has a personal history. It is up to you to value and keep it, keeping track of your information so it reflects your life satisfactorily.

Documents about a certain time and place are particularly valuable when they show multiple perspectives. The diaries of one person from a certain time can be compared to those of another, or two-way correspondence can show the thoughts of both parties. For example, in my presentations about personal papers, I show my audiences the letters sent to me by my mother when I attended college. It would be interesting one day to see if she has the letters that I sent to her. The two collections can be placed alongside each other to reflect our relationship during that time.

Professional repositories build archival collections with these connections in mind. Presenting multiple points of view, from many different angles, with many different types of materials, may better help researchers understand history. The Uncovering New Chicago Archives Project described in the text box on the previous page is one example of such an effort. [11]

---

[11] See the Uncovering New Chicago Archives Project at uncap.lib.uchicago.edu.

Individuals often give the personal papers they keep to appropriate repositories to help them build collections that relate to one another. Adding your perspective to the mix and your individual story helps cultural heritage institutions add to the historical record. Repositories all over the world hold and care for materials that once made up the personal collections of families. Historical societies in particular were created specifically to care for these types of materials. Within these institutions, the stories of famous local residents are intermingled with those of "ordinary" citizens to form a clearer picture of community.

Documents about You

To put together your own collection about your life, think of all the documentation in the world that relates to you and your place in society. Start simply and consider the materials that are most personal to you. In my case, this would be my diaries. There are also other things I have created, such as my schoolwork, artwork, the drafts of my writings, snapshots, and journals I keep about my homes and gardens. Also among the personal, but not created by me, are my health records, credit information, financial data, and other things that I consider private but that are generally kept in the hands of others. There are records about me that are considered "public" for all to see, such as

Looking More Closely at the Term "Collection"

Within a collecting repository, a collection includes all of the materials held by the institution. This term can also be used to describe individual groupings of similar materials that relate to a particular subject or idea.

Museum artifact collections such as those found at the Museum of Fine Arts (MFA) in Boston are cared for using standards that differ from archives, but objects need supporting archival documentation. The MFA has strong archives collections to support its collection of artifacts.

The whole archival collection of the MFA in Boston includes records related to the history of the museum and its objects. There are individual archival collections related to the people who worked there, the building, and the organization's activities. All of these categories of material are owned by the Museum and are part of their larger "collection" or "collections."

"Dear Diary..." (My Earliest Journal Writing)

July 1, 1982

My dad, sister, and I went fishing today. My little brother was upset because we told him we were going to the beach. So mom took him to the park and bought him a sundae. We did not catch any fish. It was pretty boring. We came home and went swimming. I learned to do a pretty good dive. We watched a sad movie about horses and a girl whose mother and father died. We stayed up until 11:00.

August 27, 2010

All of my childhood memories came flooding back when I re-read the diary I kept when I was 12.

[Even the mundane descriptions can make the past a palpable part of the present, illuminating our story and making connections among life events.]

information property records, records about donations I made to political campaigns, and items I have posted on the Internet.

Within the collections of archival material we maintain are unique documents that we create as part of the work we do. One may come across research notes, workbooks, and commendations from our professional lives among our more personal materials. Small-business owners may possess marketing documents, financial records, and other materials related to their occupation. Writers' research, scientists' notes, and artists' sketches also form part of the personal archives of people from various professions.

There are also the records that we need to keep up with our everyday lives. Bills, receipts, and warranty information are all necessary to function from day to day. Some of these items have long-term value. Others are important for the short term or have a limited time in which they are useful. We need to wade through these items individually or in groups to determine what is worth keeping and what can be discarded over time.

Papers from rotaries, art clubs, mothers' groups, and other associations can often be found among the personal papers in our homes, showing the groups in which we participate and serve. Most associations pass papers to new board members at the start of their terms. The secretary keeps her notes; the treasurer keeps financial records. Programming, publicity, and other records may get passed to various committee members or from president to president. It is common for an organization to have many decades' worth of records with no permanent home.

Some of the pieces of my individual history and the documents connecting me to the communities in which I take part are gathered tightly in my home. Some are spread in repositories where I have lived all over New York and New England. Others are sitting on remote computers around the world. Records illuminating vignettes of one's life are far flung and often reside in places we do not consider.

Figure 1. In 2010, the schoolchildren from RBS in New Hampshire thanked me for visiting them to explain about my job. They drew these pictures to show their understanding of the value of history and how it fits into their lives.

Record Life Cycle

A "record" is created for a particular purpose and is generally most actively used soon after its creation. With the passage of time, the primary purpose for which a document is created elapses, or users need to access the document less frequently.

Phases of the record life cycle for materials in the home:

- Create
- Possibly distribute (put on the Internet, mail, hand out)
- Use
- Maintain
    - Store
    - Retrieve
    - Protect
- Dispose
    - Transfer to temporary storage (for materials that need to be kept for legal reasons or items you are unsure about)
    - Destroy
    - Permanently store

Appraisal

In the archives field, the term "appraisal" most commonly refers to the process used to assess records and to determine those to keep permanently. Though we may want to, it is impractical for us to keep everything. To enhance the focus of our materials (keeping what best tells our story) and to improve accessibility to our files, it is a good idea to cull our collections for materials that follow the guidelines outlined in this section.[12]

Records have a "life." They are created for a particular reason. They are usually actively used for a relatively short period. They then should be discarded or carefully stored forever. Those who manage records professionally in the United States think about the creation, use, and disposition of documents along the record life cycle.

Once the original purpose for which a record was created has been fulfilled, we must reexamine the significance of that document. For example, one may write down information for a project. When the project ends, the documentation remains to represent the activities

---

[12] For a good appraisal tool, see New York State Archives' Appraisal of Historical Records (www.archives.nysed.gov/a/records/mr_pub50_introduction.shtml), which includes an appraisal scorecard to assist with decisions about which records to save and which to discard.

that occurred and to transfer the knowledge that resulted. This item is called an archival document because it has long-term value as evidence and information. When individuals do not think about this "record life cycle" and their reasons for retaining items, many useless materials are kept that do not possess archival value, making it difficult to organize materials and to find what we need when we need it, while muddying our personal narrative.

When we want to keep a well-rounded group of records about our lives, it is not desirable to keep everything. Keeping everything takes up valuable storage space, makes it more cumbersome to find what we need, and requires us to wade through useless and repetitive documents just to locate the "good stuff." Archivists use the process of "appraisal" to determine which materials truly have value as archives and should be kept forever.[13] Proper appraisal is based on about one hundred years of professional archives theory and practice that takes into account the various values of our materials. People with archival materials in their homes should use some of these professional concepts to enhance their personal collections.

You may know intuitively certain items that you wish to keep for personal, sentimental reasons. Items that retain value for us just because of what they are have what we call "intrinsic" value. For example, my father has a keychain with a small stereoscopic picture of himself as a boy. Because he is my father and this item

Figure 2. These objects are used by my family to view treasured family images. *Objects from the author's family collection. Photo by Esther Lowenthal.*

is unique among all of our family photos, this artifact holds intrinsic value for me. Even if we had a duplicate copy of this photo in printed form, this little keychain has special significance because I remember looking through it with my dad when I was a kid.[14]

---

[13] For a thorough discussion of appraisal, see my first book, *Cultural Heritage Collaborators: A Manual for Community Documentation.*

[14] Many of the items that hold intrinsic value for an individual would not hold the same value for an archival institution. Appraisal decisions by archivists are made based on community and history-related values. My dad's picture would have value as an item that helps tell my family story, but it would not involve the same sentimental attachment in a repository.

Sentimental Journey

Certain items are worth keeping just because of their existence. These items embody sentiment or a symbolic meaning that elevates any informational value they may hold. For example, the Declaration of Independence holds importance for its information, but that information has been duplicated many times. The original is important as evidence, showing what was truly said, without concern that it was miscopied or mistranslated over time. But it also holds importance simply as a symbol of liberty to the American people.

Within families, we possess personal symbols that represent what family means to us and our heritage. One of the most powerful personal symbols in my family is a jewel that my grandmother sewed into the lining of her clothes when she left Europe during the Holocaust. Its symbolism is more important than any monetary or informational value it may hold.

Sometimes sentimentality gets in the way and we are too close to events to properly appraise whether we should keep certain things related to them. For example, I may not have had the heart to throw away any of the papers my daughter brought home from school during first grade, but by the time she reached second grade, I was able to look at the items with a more detached frame of mind and keep only those that best reflected the work she did the previous year. Similarly, immediately after a person passes away is not the time to evaluate what is worth keeping and what should be discarded. Help loved ones appraise their materials during their lifetimes or, after a death, wait until some time passes and you are more distanced from the emotional trauma.[15]

Consider what is important to fully document that which is most representative of your life. These items provide evidence of your past or information about your day-to-day activities, personal values, and accomplishments. Such materials are ones to which you would want to refer to reminisce about your younger years, tell stories to your grandkids, or just recall the specifics about

However, there are items that do evoke a sentimental attachment to a community. Items such as the Liberty Bell, state and national constitutions, and items that belonged to historical figures (such as Abe Lincoln's hat) fit into this category.

[15] Professional organizer Sue West frequently writes eloquently in her blog "Organizing for the Next Chapter of Your Life" about "letting go." Her post "The Tales and the Evidence" (organizenh.com/wordpress/2009/11/the-tales-and-the-evidence) addresses working through emotional issues to save the objects and stories that are most important to you.

Figure 3. Ephemera, including such items as these brochures, are created for a specific one-time purpose. They may be worth saving beyond this intended short-term use as evidence of an individual or institution's activities.

things that are important to you. The evidence you retain can help you sort through problems in the future or make plans at crossroads in your life.

Get rid of items that are meant for short-term use alone and have no inherent value. Grocery lists, Post-it notes, and the like should not be kept. Other records that serve a relatively short purpose should be evaluated as such. Financial records, for one, need to be evaluated for continued usefulness.[16]

Seek to create, collect, and use your own records and memorabilia mindfully. If possible, identify materials worth saving forever as soon as you create them so that you may properly care for them right at the outset. Think about what you create that might be discarded immediately after use, so that you can make room and devote more resources to your long-term documents.[17]

The value of your personal materials often becomes most clear when you are trying to "process" your collections. This is when you actually sit down with a box of materials to organize, preserve, and describe them. These functions are discussed in more detail in later chapters. Pertinent to the discussion of appraisal, know that you must make decisions about what to keep and what to discard when considering the bulk of items *and* when working to organize individual groupings of documents. Organizing collections helps you determine if you have duplicate copies, similar items, and unrelated records that you may not know about when considering your collection on a larger scale.

---

[16] Many CPAs place useful information online about how long to keep financial records. For one such list, see the FSO Technologies Inc. "Recordkeeping Guide: How Long Should You Retain Your Records?" (fso.cpasitesolutions.com/Premium/LE/21_le_ot/fg/fg-Record_Keeping.html).

[17] The field of "records management" deals with managing active and semi-active records that may not have long-term value. For more information, see "Paper Management: Organizing and Preserving Important Document and Items" (librarysupportstaff.com/papermngt.html).

Personal Timeline

List the important people, places, and events in your life. As an example, below I list some of the memorable things I associate with a period in my life that I want to document. Lists like this can also be saved to become an important part of your documentation.

<u>High School</u>

- Teachers—especially those who influenced me, such as Mr. Panek (history).
- Friends—Suzie (early high school), Debbie (later). Prom. Coming out of my shell senior year.
- Track and cross-country. First time I made county championships. Seven-mile race when I won unicorn statue. My coach, Mr. Zimmers. Dad attending my meets.
- Summer School of the Arts in Buffalo, junior year—photography, first boyfriend.

When considering your personal archives, identify the materials that may be important to a larger community outside of your family. Seek unique records that provide informational or intrinsic value worth retaining. Records that shed light on the role your family has played in society are particularly noteworthy. Consider all of the possible subjects that are reflected in your papers. List the communities in which your family has taken part, and consider what communities might be interested in particular subjects.[18] Consult a professional archivist in your community to help you determine if your items provide valuable information for researchers, filling a gap in the existing historical record and matching a community need for information. Certain items may be appropriate for deposit in a repository.

Appraisal is an art, not a science. As part of appraisal, make a list of the important people, places, and events in the course of your life that your personal collection should mention. You can even devise a timeline listing important events. Evaluate available existing documentation in your home and in the homes of your loved ones. Identify gaps in your materials. This knowledge can be used to actively shape your personal collections. Be careful not to discard unique or enlightening items that provide vital evidence of the activities and functions of an individual or group, but do not be afraid to get rid of items that do not provide strong information about an aspect of your life that should be documented. Seek elucidating information. Get rid of the clutter.

---

[18] See page 23 for a list of communities.

The next section discusses the common personal archives, which serve as documentation of the things in your life and should be included as part of your personal narrative.

Common Personal Archives

This section focuses more on the types of documents we retain to help you with the process of determining what to keep and what to discard. It focuses on the common personal archives you may find in your home. It helps you identify the materials that should be saved for posterity by discussing the value of each type.

I begin with photographs, which are perhaps the most widespread among personal documents found in homes. First, individuals have an immediate emotional reaction when they view loved ones in photos, and they therefore tend to place more value in photos than in other documentation. Photographs can tell us a lot about how individuals looked, but they can also reveal information about the environment in which they lived. They greatly enhance personal narrative and understanding of an individual's life. However, the historical worth of these materials diminishes greatly when images are unlabeled and the people or places within the images cannot be identified.

Archives Versus Artifact

Archives are a type of artifact. Both artifacts and archives are man-made objects that are similarly valued for historical reasons. However, archives are generally accepted as two-dimensional, while artifacts are three-dimensional. (Exceptions to this are objects such as drawings, which more often than not are grouped with artifacts. There are, indeed, many shades of gray, and the collections of archivists and curators often overlap.) Most professional Archives focus primarily on collections of the written or spoken word, while artifacts are appreciated for their form. Archives can and should be used to enhance the value of artifacts, providing written documentation that describes the context of material so that it is better understood.

Communication Tools: Are You Listening (And Taking Note)?

For a while, every few weeks I would get a voicemail from my four-year-old niece. It went like this: "Hello? Helloooo! HELLOOO!! Hello?"

Miriam is reaching out through a very impermanent communication tool. The telephone generally allows us to express a thought, transferring the idea to someone else without recording it for posterity. However, there are times when this tool crosses into the realm of archives, such as when my niece leaves me a recording that I want to save to remember my funny phone calls. I can save the recording and keep it as part of my personal archives, with a note explaining its context, of course.

Also among the most exciting archival resources in personal collections are diaries. Diaries can reveal a lot about a person and the events surrounding that person's life. Individuals who have old diaries from ancestors are lucky to possess remarkable pieces of historical information that are especially compelling because of their private nature. A diary can be an indicator of personal growth, showing how an individual worked out problems. (I sometimes use my own diaries as a reference tool to look back over my life and see how far I have come and how much I have learned.) Diaries often reveal an individual's thoughts that may not have been expressed in any other format. These items have strong sentimental value for family members, but they also have historical value beyond the family. The stories of Martha Ballard and Anne Frank are two well-known examples that illustrate how remarkable and noteworthy a diary can be for history.[19]

---

[19] Beginning in the 1950s, many historians turned their attention from the stories of prominent white men to focus their studies on everyday people. They began digging in archives and homes looking for papers that elicited information about the activities of wide groups of Americans to create a "people's history." The work of social historians seeks to show how masses of people and the ways they lived their daily lives influenced events and the development of American society. The discovery of Ballard's diary in a New England collection and the subsequent writing of a book about it by Laurel Thatcher Ulrich did much to change our impression of the role and day-to-day lives of eighteenth-century women. Ulrich, Laurel Thatcher, *A Midwife's Tale: The Life of Martha Ballard Based on Her Diary, 1785–1812* (New York: Alfred A. Knopf, Inc., 1990).

Health records, financial records, and the materials we create in our "official" everyday activities often have long-term value. When considering these items, it is important to try to distinguish those that fill short-term needs from archives. For example, a prescription from your doctor is immediately handed to a pharmacist, but the notes your doctor takes about your illness are kept protected among the doctor's records to help with your future health and could even one day be used by a researcher studying various health issues. Likewise, a receipt for a pair of socks you bought is no longer needed once you have decided not to return the item, whereas your mortgage information will be kept until your home is paid off or even longer to document your house history.

Correspondence is one of the most interesting forms of archival material. People retain old written letters from friends and family, personal notes and greetings, and formal letters in file boxes and cabinets. These documents tell us much about people's relationships and communities.[20] It is important to realize that this kind of communication is changing rapidly, and we must now also be aware of what electronic messages we might want to save for the long term. Though archival repositories once had difficulty gathering collections

Cookbooks as Personal History

I write in my cookbooks. I record my changes to recipes. I make notes about which members of my family like certain recipes and which do not. The holidays at which I serve certain foods are mentioned. On some recipes, I write down a memory about when I served the food. All of these notes make my book something a little more personal than the average cookbook. It becomes more than just a mass-produced item. It tells something about me and my family. A cookbook can fill a unique place in a family archive, describing a part of our culture that is often not recorded. It provides a more rounded view of our life. In a later chapter, I discuss how you can use information such as this to enhance documentation about your family, adding to it and making your personal story more significant to others.

---

[20] For a wonderful example of correspondence documenting a life-long relationship see, ed. Emily Herring Wilson, *Two Gardeners: Katharine S. White and Elizabeth Lawrence—A Friendship in Letters* (Boston: Beacon Press, 2002).

of back-and-forth correspondence, today computers retain both sides of a conversation. Additionally, where once our correspondence was private, usually sent from us to one recipient, more and more often we are sending messages out to many people at a time through e-mail and social networking sites. In fact, we often send correspondence out to total strangers, changing the way we think about privacy. Furthermore, as we share more about ourselves in this way, we write fewer and fewer words in one shot to do it. And because social networks and e-mail are virtually free, we can make use of them with tools that are available to us at any time. This gives us the tendency to write in shorter bursts and more often than in the past. No matter the form our writing takes, we need to consider our communiqués as a whole, recognizing them as unique and valuable to our personal narrative.

Another revealing type of material found in personal collections is published resources. Archives are distinct from books and other publications because they are unique documents and are not mass-produced. However, there are publications that may have value as "archives," embodying something unique that makes them one-of-a-kind. Cookbooks and recipe cards with personal notes

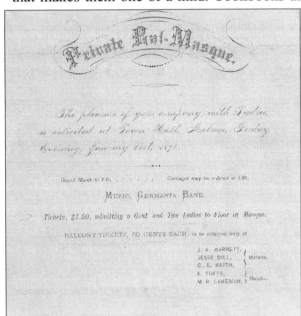

written in by the family chef, family bibles with recorded births and deaths, and books with marginalia revealing the impressions of the reader may all have value as archival resources. Often, the personalized information cannot be found easily elsewhere. These items may get passed from generation to generation because of their distinct qualities.

Generally, mass-produced or published items are called "secondary sources" and are not kept in archival collections. Unique manuscripts, or what professionals consider "archival" material, are "primary sources." Secondary sources are usually

Figure 4. This invitation requests the pleasure of the recipient's company. The receiver saved the ephemeral document after it served its intended purpose, and it is now a useful piece of history.

one step removed from the person or event they depict. They are written by event outsiders who may or may not have a direct connection with the related activity. Although secondary sources may be valuable research tools, they are not the firsthand accounts tied most closely to the circumstance considered and created by an authoritative source. We sometimes may keep secondary sources, but their value for our personal history generally lies in our sentimental attachment or in the way they help add meat to our story. For example, books written by authors that are retained in the author's collections can help us better understand that writer's life. When I worked as an archivist in Waltham, Massachusetts, our archives retained the books of F. Lee Bailey—well-known attorney, author, and former Waltham resident—to mark his role in our community history and help tell the story of our city. The significance of such materials should be fully explained for future generations to understand why they are valuable to our personal narrative.

Among our collections, we do oftentimes care for ephemeral items as archival material, even though they are created en masse to provide information for an event. Ephemeral items are not created to survive indefinitely, but instead are made to serve a short-term purpose. They include things such as brochures, cards, flyers, tickets, and pamphlets. Ephemera can be historically enlightening and are often rare, if not unique, because of their intended short-term purpose and our tendency to easily dispose of them.

Maya Angelou's Personal Papers

On the day that I am writing this, the Schomburg Center for Research in Black Culture, part of the New York Public Library, announced its acquisition of Maya Angelou's personal papers. The collection includes notes she kept to write her books, personal and professional correspondence, and other records that reveal the writer's life and work. I expect the items reveal much about the famed persona and also tell us something about Angelou as a woman representative of others who grew up in the segregated South in the mid-twentieth century. Every collection, whether related to the famous or not-so-famous, has multiple angles and multiple audiences who can learn from the stories that archives reveal.

Personalized greeting cards straddle the world of archives, ephemera, and secondary sources. Created en masse, these items often have a unique quality that ties them to an individual. Yet they are generally intended to relate a sentiment for a particular occasion and not necessarily meant to serve as keepsakes. Greeting cards can be useful informational resources if they relate the feelings of one individual to another, give us clues about important events in individuals' lives, and demonstrate larger trends evident in their style. Some cards may also not contain any historical value whatsoever if they lack personalization or contain a bland message.

Yearbooks are another type of material readily found in homes, but they are created in bulk. They are unique because though they are mass-produced, they contain information that ties directly to one's life and include photographs and printed personal reminiscences that evoke memories of a particular time and place. Yearbooks also often contain unique handwritten sentiments of classmates that give additional clues about an individual's educational experiences and relationships. People treasure yearbooks for the memories they evoke and the details they provide about the way a person looked, dressed, and acted during formative years of his life.

Scrapbooks are commonly found in personal collections. Each is unique in that the materials within its pages were chosen and organized by individuals aiming to highlight something important to them. Most scrapbooks contain news clippings, which are not unique in themselves, but it can often be difficult to track down the individual pieces of news that here are gathered neatly in one place. In addition to its news clippings, scrapbooks often contain other mementos from an individual's life, recalling valued memories.

There is a fine line between different types of cultural heritage materials. We often find ephemera and published material mixed in with archival material. It is important to understand distinctions so we understand the context under which our information is created, helping us make better decisions about how we will use and care for our documented information.[21]

---

[21] Different types of cultural items have different needs for their care. Later chapters discuss differing organizational and preservation techniques.

Saving Our Things

Joan asked me to help her with her family papers. She had materials of her own that documented her years in public school, her religious education, and correspondence from a boyfriend. She had old fashion magazines that she looked through with her grandmother when she was young. Her collection included old comic books, many with the covers ripped off, that she had collected as a child. She also had the papers of her parents, including letters to her mother from an aunt who had emigrated from Europe. Joan had never known her aunt, and these were the first materials she considered disposing. The letters talked about life and struggles in the new country. I convinced Joan to give these a second look, to cherish them as a piece of her heritage or donate them to a local historical society that collected heavily in the area of immigration. I told Joan to consider getting rid of the magazines and comics since they are not primary materials and are duplicated in many libraries. Joan's memories that are connected to those items are strong, however, and instead she chose to keep them. I suggested that she write a little paragraph to retain with the materials to discuss how they are important to her, making them a more meaningful part of her collection to future generations.

Example: The Value of Personal Memorabilia

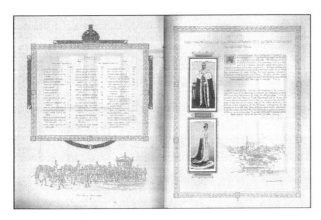

Figure 5. Cigarette trading cards from author's personal collection of ephemera.

I found this book while vacationing in Bermuda. It possesses sentimental value related to my trip but has little monetary worth. It is interesting as an historical item, but it was produced en masse and is not unique.

A cigarette trading card book such as this possesses collectible value. Such books also have some historical value as pieces that highlight the interests of society in a certain time and place. This particular example, made to commemorate the coronation of King George VI, served as a memento of the occasion. Cards aimed to advertise a company while using popular subjects that appealed to specific groups at which the company's product was aimed. As collecting cards became popular, so did the idea of books that could contain them as keepsakes. My book is also a beautiful work of art, with sketches representative of England and rich colors in the portraits. There are repositories that collect such items. The largest collection of cigarette trading cards is purported by Wikipedia to be held at the British Museum.

For me, the value of this item is in the memory it elicits of a special event in my life. I remember the fun I had on the trip, the comfort of being with my husband, the interest I had in the little shop where this was found, and the excitement I felt at connecting with something that is tied to a personal interest of mine (English history). The book reminds me of a place and time, bringing up warm feelings. One of the reasons that people surround themselves with such memorabilia is so that those feelings of a moment last into the future. The items we choose to keep tell something about us—our interests and what we value—and for these reasons, the items may hold long-term purpose in our personal archives.

Sample Collection: The Ryans of Waltham

While working as the archivist at the Waltham Public Library in Massachusetts, I took in a collection of papers related to one of the biggest celebrations Waltham ever saw. In the 1990s, in an attempt to document the town and to raise community pride, the "Watch City" launched its *Waltham Rediscovered* project. Town residents participated in separate parties celebrating the heritages of Waltham's many immigrant groups. People brought photos, documents, and objects to these events that showed their family history and their community roots. The celebrations culminated in the writing of a book that stands as a testimonial of the diversity of Waltham's populace.

I accessioned the research papers related to the project for the library. Among the materials that the project coordinator/historian had gathered with her volunteers were some of the personal papers loaned by city residents. These materials were given so they could be duplicated for publication, but no formal written agreements had been signed that would give the project the rights to keep the materials. I set about procuring the signatures I needed to make this a proper donation. This would allow library patrons to view and use the items with the blessings of the individuals whose papers were included in the collection.

Among the *Waltham Rediscovered* materials were papers from Waltham's Ryan family. Albert M. Ryan II and his twin brother, Henry, had deep roots in the Waltham community. Family members had lived in town for generations. My box of materials included postcards, photos, and drawings of Albert Ryan I, who was a city employee and town historian. I wrote to the brothers and asked if they wished to have the materials from *Waltham Rediscovered* returned or if they would like to make a home for them at the library. I asked if they would sign some papers granting the repository formal permission for the materials' keeping and use.

Mr. Albert Ryan's response to me began a yearlong correspondence that introduced one of the most interesting collections of family papers that I have encountered and one of the nicest library patrons I have ever met. Mr. Ryan wrote that he was in the process of sorting through his papers. He wanted me to keep what I had and indicated he had more to bring. At 82 and after the recent death of his twin brother, he wrote, he wanted to pass his things on. I expected more materials from the town historian and, indeed, his notebooks and scrapbooks were included among the materials I was later given. But there was more from many

Figure 6. Henry M. Ryan II served in the Civil War and wrote letters home to his mother. Image courtesy of Waltham Public Library.

generations of Ryans.

The Ryans had not only lived in Waltham for a long time—family members also participated in recognizable activities that marked major historical events in American history. Through the Ryan papers, we get a strong sense of the passing of generations and what it was like to be born in Waltham among many generations of a family that stayed rooted there. The city had been the birthplace of the Industrial Revolution, though that title in common knowledge has been displaced by the city of Lowell. Lowell was established a decade later, further north on a faster-flowing river that was more conducive to the textile work of Waltham's entrepreneurs. When we think of the city of Waltham, we still think of those industrial roots.

Mr. Ryan brought me items that he himself had carefully labeled. He identified who was in pictures and who wrote documents. He described the relationships between his family members. He also noted his memories about certain places in Waltham that no longer existed or the role a place played in his life. He sat and talked to me and answered questions I had about his family and their relationships. I recorded his responses in my accession records—the official papers archivists keep when taking in new collections.

Mr. Ryan gave the library the letters of Henry M. Ryan I, his great-grandfather, who participated in the Gold Rush and wrote home to his family. Mr. Ryan also gave us the letters of Henry Ryan II, who served in the Civil War and wrote home to his mother. Ida Annah Ryan's papers were of particular interest to a young professional archivist with a feminist college mentor. Ms. Ryan was our donor's aunt. She was the first woman to receive a master's degree from MIT, was a renowned architect, and was an active suffragette.

Here is the transcript from a sample document:

October 30, 1852

Dear Brother:

I wrote you a letter on the 13th instant I then told you that I was going to the mind and I went but they did[n't] prove to my likeing [sic] and so I have returned to this place and have gone to work at Carpenter work at $7.00 per day...

...See how the folks get a long and write to me all the news that you can find and see that they have all they want if you can find it for them without injury to yourself if I have my health I shall be able to repay you shortly...

Nine months later, Henry's brother received a letter that his Henry had been ill for about two weeks and then passed away.

I wrote to Mr. Ryan, "Your donation is quite a valuable addition to the Library.... The Ryans play such a vital role in this City's consciousness. Researchers and others interested in Waltham will be very happy to have access to the documents of your ancestors."

The records of other families in Waltham show what it was like to live among diverse immigrant populations. Taken together, these collections give a broad scope of life in the city, how it has changed over time, and how Waltham reflects changes in American culture in general. From the long-lived resident Ryan family to transient immigrants who helped shape the city's industrial roots, the records of Waltham's families in the public library, in the historical society, and the museum help preserve the history of urban development. Documenting growth while highlighting Waltham's historical place, personal papers form the backbone of community memory.

From Mr. Ryan, I learned the value of an archivist reaching out and forming bonds with members of the community. My professional life and the collections I kept benefited from my meeting Mr. Ryan and the work we did to transfer his collection to the library over several months. I also gained much on a personal level from an elderly gentleman willing to share his family history with a young archivist. Together we helped to weave his story into the written record of Waltham and to deepen our own personal understandings of community.[22]

Figure 7. Albert M. Ryan I served as Waltham historian and worked in local government. He is pictured here with grandsons Henry Ryan III and Albert M. Ryan II. Albert M. Ryan II donated his personal papers and those of his family to the Waltham Public Library. *Image courtesy Waltham Public Library.*

---

[22] Learn more about the Ryan family collection in "A Collection and Its Donor," *ArchivesInfo* newsletter, December 2009, www.archivesinfo.com/newsletter/December2009.pdf (July 27, 2011).

Mental and Writing Exercises for Identifying Archives

1. List the types of archives you have in your home.

2. Name other places where records about you are housed. (Think about town government records, school records, medical records, etc.)

3. Identify family members and friends that are well represented in your collections. Do any of them have information about you that you do not have recorded in your own collections? Do they provide a different and useful perspective on your personal narrative?

4. Pick one aspect of your life and create a timeline listing the important people, places, and events from that time. (See text box on page 50 for my high school list as an example)

5. What personal symbols do you own that represent your life and your heritage? Have you recorded information about what makes these items special?

6. Do you keep notes in your family cookbook? Do you write in the margins of your books? Do you keep a scrapbook with seemingly random news clippings? Consider what secondary resources in your possession help define your life. Make a list of five secondary sources that tell something about you. If their importance needs explaining, write a paragraph describing how it helps define your narrative.

7. Do you keep "everything" in fear of discarding something "valuable"? Identify a few items you can now remove from your personal files.

Chapter Three:
Organizing Archives

Start Where You Are—Everything Can Be Organized

Some of us are born with an innate interest and ability to organize. I understood that when my daughter lined up crayons by color on the first step of our home when she was ten months old. It came naturally to her, just as it comes to me. Those of us who have the "librarian gene," as my mother fondly calls it, have been known to figure out the best methods of organization for a multitude of items just for kicks. In fact, my husband has grown accustomed to coming home to find the furniture rearranged; I'll say, "I thought it would 'work' better this way, honey."

You may not be like me, but here you are reading this book, with a keen interest in organizing your collection. There are standard methods for organization that others have thought up for you. No matter how disorganized you feel, remember that everything can be organized to some useful degree. Start with a small selection of your things and give it order. It does not matter where you start: There is no beginning, middle, and end.

Thinking about Order

The purpose of organizing your personal materials is to give them a structure that makes it easy for you to use them. Your goal is to establish an order that makes sense to you for the items that you will keep permanently. The organizational scheme for your own items should fit your lifestyle and sensibilities. There is no correct way to organize. In fact, there are always multiple ways to systematize a collection. Determine what works best for you. Use basic archives principles and rules of thumb with help from examples provided in this chapter to make your work easier.

Return to the idea of thinking of your personal papers as a collection representing your life. If possible, aim to centralize your materials. Is it even possible to keep them all in one room? (Call it your "Personal Archives" room.) Keeping organized things together makes it easier to conceptualize it as a collection. With bits of your life brought between four walls, a ceiling, and floor, the room becomes like a giant box for keeping your archives and molding your life story.

Once the bulk of the records in your home are together in a room (or if you cannot get them all together, once you have identified your personal "collection" spread throughout your home), you need to think about this collection in terms of smaller groups. Organizing records into logical record units enhances their accessibility.[23] Unlike our museum and library colleagues' predominant organizing techniques, archivists examine materials in groupings rather than working with single items. Documents as part of larger collections tell us more about history than individual items. Our ultimate goal is to think about our personal papers as a contained source of information about our life and our activities. We aim to keep things organized to highlight the valuable information that tells our stories.

Processing Records

This section considers the organization of your records with permanent value as opposed to records we keep for the short term. Organizing these records is part of the procedure we call "processing." Together with preservation and description, arrangement is a fundamental part of preparing archival materials for use, and all are part of the processing practice. An archivist ensures that collections are neat and have a fundamental categorized structure. During the process of ensuring an understandable arrangement, the archivist fixes preservation problems and notes important elements of the collection. We perform all of the aspects of processing at once, returning later to add details

Figure 8. The process of organizing archives. Put series of papers into folders and archival boxes. A box is your number-one tool for the order and protection of your records.

---

[23] The groupings we use are called "fonds" or "record groups," which refer to a large body of related records kept together based on their origin or provenance (i.e., where they came from and who created them.) We also note "series," which denote smaller grouping of records within the fonds. For example, a series may be someone's journals or the materials related to a particular event such as a wedding.

and to perfect our work. This book discusses the larger idea of processing in more detail in later chapters.

Figure 9. Everything can be organized. Pick a box. If necessary, bring it to a clean room so you do not have to see—and be overwhelmed by—the rest of the collection.

Processing = Arranging + Preserving + Describing

Provenance

When organizing in an institution, professionals try to keep together all records of the same origin. Known as maintaining "provenance," this means that the personal papers of a donor are kept together rather than separated in favor of some archivist-imposed system. In fact, archivists generally name collections after the person or institution that created its contents. Following the principle of provenance in your home means that you must keep your papers separate and distinct from those of others that have been passed down to you and from those of other family members. Furthermore, each collection should be valued as a whole and not for its separate parts whenever possible. In other words, keep groups of materials together, rather than pulling out and separately storing individual documents that seem important or interesting. Instead, make note of interesting materials and of connections between separate collections.[24]

Recently, I was watching a popular antiques show.[25] A woman brought in materials that had been passed down through her family. The original owner of the collection was a relative who attended a Native American school. The collection included a diploma and other school materials of the main person associated with the collection, but it also included signed photos of famous sports figures who had attended the school, too. Together these materials tell a unique story. The fact that the items were kept together for one hundred years is significant. Some of these materials on their own are valuable, but the story about how they came to this particular collection make them even more desirable and interesting.

---

[24] Throughout this chapter I allude to taking notes and making indices. These processes are explained in more detail in the next chapter.
[25] "Carlisle Indian School Archive, ca. 1910," *Antiques Roadshow*, aired May 23, 2011, www.pbs.org/wgbh/roadshow/archive/201006A09.html (July 27, 2011).

Original Order

We learn a lot about a person's thought process by seeing how that person organized his papers. In addition to maintaining the records' provenance, we try to keep the order the person applied to his collection. The Salman Rushdie archives on page 193 provides a good example of why this is valuable. We see how the famous author came up with his ideas. We better understand his workflow. We can consider things such as how his work habits made him successful, how he makes connections between ideas, how he is like us, and how he is different. His means of gathering, creating, and maintaining information can be as enlightening as the product he shows us in the end.

If one day you pass your records on to someone else, they should be kept in the order you impose. This holds true for materials that were passed down to you by another family member. Retain them in the order in which they were received if there is any sense to that order at all. Another order may make better sense to us, but we should not rearrange materials to impose our own organizational sensibilities.[26] Here's another way to look at it: Do not make extra work for yourself. If something already has an order to it, keep it that way.

Figure 10. Retain the materials passed to you from others in the order in which you receive them.

For your own materials, providing an organizational scheme makes it easier for you to find what you need, and it also helps anyone else dealing with the papers in the future. Taking notes about your actions helps you later describe your materials so others can access items should you choose to pass them on to a family member or repository. Record information about your organizational decisions. Write why you chose the arrangement methods you put in place.[27]

---

[26] Archivists create written indices that "intellectually" rearrange the collection to conform to our preferred organizational means. This is discussed more in a later chapter. We try to adhere to the principle of "sanctity of original order," which states that the original order should be retained whenever possible.

[27] In a formal repository, comments about the organization are noted in an "Arrangement" note within a manuscript inventory or finding aid. Chapter Four discusses these access tools in greater detail.

When working with records given to you by someone else, begin by reviewing the entire collection. Do not rearrange anything. Use this preliminary review to familiarize yourself with the materials and to prepare for the next steps. Take notes on a pad or with cards. Document how you found the collection. Note the order of the materials. Record dates, highlights of the collection, and any noteworthy information you find.

If (and only if) the collection is, by your estimation, totally disorganized, develop a processing plan. This plan is an outline describing the groupings of materials you think you might employ to help you work out an organizational scheme. Do you have lots of materials from particular dates? Do you have materials written by certain people? Do materials describe certain events?

Basic Arrangement Dos and Don'ts

- DO NOT try to organize and describe collections item by item
- DO organize and describe your materials in series groupings

- DO NOT separate materials created by someone else that come to you as a single collection
- DO retain the provenance of materials, keeping items together to reflect the creator of the collection

- DO NOT intermingle materials from different creators or donors
- DO keep materials separate and note connections between materials in a finding aid (as described in the next chapter)

- DO NOT rearrange materials that were given an arrangement by their creator
- DO keep the order imposed by the creator of the collection to reflect that person's thought process

Identifying Series Groups

I find "surveying" records to be one of the handiest methods for reviewing collection materials. I generally survey large collections that are spread over institutions, but the method is useful for reviewing all of the materials in your home or just a box of papers in front of you. As you browse through papers, make a quick list of what you find. You will start to see connections among materials. This list can serve to help you identify the types of materials you have. It can help you later create an index to your materials if they are organized. It can help you plan out how to organize your materials if they are disorganized. Aim to identify groupings when you can, rather than noting materials item-by-item. Below is a sample of my survey notes for a project. On just this one page, you can see how the records related to finance, workshops, and exhibits are outstanding. This list helped me create an appropriate organizational scheme for those materials that lacked one.

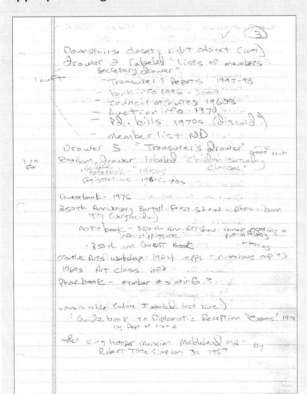

Figure 11. Writing down some information about the materials in front of you can help you spot logical groupings for unarranged records.

The Value of Original Order

Very often, any order possessed by documents is destroyed before they reach a professional repository. Well-meaning individuals try to reorganize materials to make it easier to access items. Or, sometimes, after materials are donated to a less professional facility, the semi-professional or volunteer in charge of archives will pull apart any structure given to a group of records by its creator to arrange items by subject across many record groups. This was the case when I was given the job as the first professional archivist of the Waltham Public Library in Massachusetts. In Waltham, I created some "record groups" based on subjects (not the preferable method) because no evidence of who created or donated the records in a fifty-year-old collection was left. Furthermore, many pieces of the collection were donated as individual items, leaving no way to organize in groupings unless I artificially made them. But as I settled into my job and began collecting more materials, I began asking people to donate true "natural" collections that retained the order given to them by their creator. Natural collections stand in contrast to "artificial" ones where someone has rearranged materials in multiple collections to impose a scheme that the organizer thinks is better. In Waltham, I began naming records groups using labels such as "Albert Ryan Collection" instead of "Main Street." Although it is useful to be able to pull "Main Street" materials out of a "Main Street" box, we lose any presence of the person who created the collection to accomplish a subject arrangement. We also lose informational value when we split collections donated intact or allow collections of personal papers to be donated in pieces. The organizer of a collection should create a "finding aid" or index to a whole collection to help one access materials about Main Street in different boxes and to retain personal papers as a contained source of information about a life. Avoid the temptation to rearrange family files that are not your own when they already have a structure.

Grouping Records in Record Units

Item—It is rare that one document stands alone in an Archives. Records reveal most about history when they are placed in context with other items.

Series—A series is a small grouping of records that have a similar theme, result from the same activity, or have similar formats. Series form the major organizational structure of a collection. Subseries are smaller divisions within a series that can be useful for further categorization.

Record groups (also known as fonds)—This is the largest grouping of materials generally used for applying order to collections. It includes materials kept together based on their origin (i.e., provenance). In your home, record groups may be represented by different people— e.g., my papers versus my husband's papers.

Collection—This is a term used to describe large related groupings of materials. It can describe materials related to a single record group or many records groups put together: e.g., "Melissa's Collection" or "The Mannon Family Collection."

Levels of Arrangement

Archivists consider "levels of arrangement," which encourage us to begin thinking about a collection in a broad context. We then move on to consider various parts of the whole. When creating your processing plan for a disorganized collection of materials, identify whether your large groupings of materials can be arranged by subject, type of document, or a chronology. Then, think about how large groupings can be broken down into smaller ones. For example, can correspondence be broken down by correspondent or date? Within my correspondence, I have created folders with the names of the people who have written to me. I could also have done this grouping by date, but I personally find that I like to look through a grouping of letters by one friend or family member at a time.

A group of files or documents can be maintained together as a unit because they are related to a particular subject or function, result from the same activity, or have a common form. Smaller groupings of materials are usually identified by a common filing order, common subject matter, or common physical type (e.g., correspondence, minutes, receipts, and drawings). Thinking on this smaller level is particularly important because it expresses the character of the collection, emphasizing certain aspects of materials that we find important. For example, my own personal materials are arranged by correspondence, business papers, photographs, schooling, memorabilia, and my daughter's papers. (Her papers, when she is old enough, will split off and become a new record group in its own right, standing as her own collection that she will likely take with her someday.) These materials form a structure for the story of my life. To me, it made sense to emphasize the activities in which I take part and the people involved rather than viewing my life on a timeline, as what I value has remained relatively constant through my life. If I chose a chronological format, instead of highlighting the consistencies, I would likely be highlighting major changes such as going off to school, getting married, having a child, etc. This would change the collection's character and would make me, and others who view the collection, think about my life

Sample box label

Record Group = Melissa Mannon
Series = College Years

Sample folder label

Subseries = "Correspondence from Mom—
College Years"
1988-1992   Folder 1 of 10

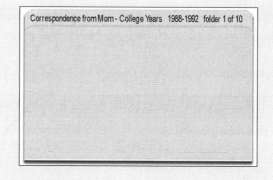

Record Groups and Series

A "record group" is a large set of documents. Any large set can be broken down into smaller sets called "series." The person who arranges a collection determines the organizational structure of the materials within that collection. Record groups are often determined based on the creator of the records, but they can be structured around types or subjects of papers.

For example, within a collection of personal papers, one may find property records. The series within that record group may include mortgage and deed, plot plans, property tax records, and household purchases.

in a different way.

When thinking of your own materials that you want to keep for posterity, start by thinking big and breaking your own collections into groupings similar to mine. Think about what groupings make sense to you based on how much of each type of material you have. Start with large sets and break into smaller subsets as often as it is desirable to you. Once you start struggling to think of a way to further break things down, you are done. Do not break the group down any further. It is okay to have "Correspondence from Mom—College Years" fill a whole box. Series

Also consider how much time you want to put into this. The most important thing is to set up records into easily understandable and accessible groupings. One of the main things about which you should be concerned is getting through everything rather than focusing on details. You can always go back and break the groupings down more if you have the time or inclination at a later date. The more you break down the groupings, the easier access should become. It is not necessary to break small groups down into even smaller components if the desired access has been achieved. Knowing it will take you about one minute to look for a document, versus thirty seconds if you broke the groups down further, will probably not make it desirable to put more work into the arrangement process.

Physical Rearrangement of Materials

When arranging your own personal papers, always remember that they are *your* materials. I reiterate that the arrangement should fit your needs and make you comfortable with using and retrieving your items. After you have carefully considered the best possible arrangements during a planning stage, you may begin to physically rearrange your own materials if you wish. You can use these same procedures for a family member's material in your care that comes to you in disarray.

During this process, you also begin to think about how you will describe your collection to make materials more accessible in the future. These notes, like the others I described earlier, help you create an index later on. Note important aspects of the collection, such as dates, strengths, and weaknesses. For example, strengths may include topics for which you have a lot of materials; weaknesses might include missing dates of records. Note interesting aspects of the collection that caught your eye while sifting through papers that may shed light on the materials. Use your personal knowledge to note connections between materials.

Record notes about sensitive subject matter, such as personal journals or financial records. Certain materials may be useful for understanding the life of a person, but you may want to keep it private for a certain period. Some records contain private information that may be unintentionally hurtful to someone. Keeping track of such records can prevent the information from ending up in places that you do not want it.

Figure 12. Organize, re-folder, and make notes about a collection at the same time.

As you rearrange materials, begin to preserve items by re-foldering and reboxing, if necessary. Within each box that you maintain, keep groupings of materials in folders so that they are neat and orderly. Folders are most often arranged chronologically, alphabetically by record creator, and by type of material (such as correspondence, photographs, and financial records.) "Mom's Correspondence" may take up a whole box, but the materials may be within ten folders arranged chronologically.

Tips to Begin Organizing Your Personal Archives

- If possible, set aside a space in your home for organization so you can sit down to work at a moment's notice when you have some free time, rather than having a need to set up and clean up each time.
- Glance through your materials and take notes before you begin physical sorting of materials. Include observations about types of records, subjects, and dates.
- Evaluate what arrangement makes sense to you based on patterns you see in the material. Decide on a chronological, alphabetical, or another organizational system.
- Keep common archives supplies on hand so you have them when you need them. Order archives boxes and folders before physical organization work begins.
- When you begin physical sorting, if you feel overwhelmed by the amount of materials in front of you, set a timer. Try working for fifteen minutes at a time, making it a goal to do a little every day.

On the left of the folder, record a title describing the series title that indicates the subject or type of materials it contains. For example, this title may say "Correspondence" or "Financial Records." On the right, record the dates included within the folder. Number the folders if there is more than one in a series (e.g., write "1 of 2").

The sorting does not have to be completed all at once. Try to set aside a space in your home so the work can continue without the need for you to set up and clean up each time you want to dive in and do a little sorting. Work in small portions of time if you want to.[28] Once you get through initial planning and sorting of large groups, focus on one section at a time and put the other materials in separate temporary homes. Archival boxes are helpful for this, or you can make piles of papers in a safe spot where they will not be disturbed. For example, create a box for correspondence, one for financials, and one for family history. Place all your materials related to a particular subject in its appropriate box with the intention of returning to that box later to sort into smaller groupings and folders. If you find yourself overwhelmed by a subject, move on

---

[28] Professional organizer Sue West of Space4U Organizing (OrganizeNH.com) recommends setting a timer to approach your work in small pieces at a time. It is reasonable to try to tackle the work in fifteen-minute increments rather than putting aside hours at a time to accomplish this.

to another one. The time one takes to get through records varies from person to person. Do not feel rushed, but set goals. If something feels tedious, move to a different portion of the collection or decide whether you are getting caught up with individual items and are not considering a larger perspective instead.

Avoid every archivist's temptation: Do not stop to read everything thoroughly. Get an idea of what the material is about, organize a section appropriately, and move on to another section. Reading through the whole collection is a treat that you can take as a reward when your processing work is complete. Finally, if you do get overwhelmed, realize that there are archives and records management consultants who can help you.

Organization involves setting up an effective system and sticking to it. Do not be afraid to organize: Just jump in and do it. As you organize, things seem to fall into place. Stay attuned to your own work habits and discover what methods fit your personality to make things easier on yourself. That's what organization is all about! If you are organized, it means that you can find what you need without anxiety. It is what you think of your system that counts. If the organization of your archives gives you easy and efficient access to your personal information, especially years down the road, you are doing it correctly.

Sorting Kids' Work

A friend recently asked me for tips on sorting the schoolwork of his two sons. He currently keeps the materials in crates. This example shows how anything can be sorted using the techniques in this chapter, regardless of the medium. Separate each child's work. Consider a chronological arrangement by school year. I keep my daughter's standard-sized work in boxes organized by grade with a separate folder for artwork each year and a separate folder behind each grade for the "work" she does outside of the classroom. I also have separate oversized folders and a box for art that does not fit in the original box. This, too, is organized by year. Remember, boxes come in any size and shape you can imagine. Keep the organization scheme simple and make the best use of the supplies available to you, keeping materials safe, unfolded, and neat. I keep only the materials I like best or that are best representative of her work over the year. One final tip: Sometimes I need to go back to weed materials a year later, when I have less sentimental attachment to them— otherwise, I would likely keep everything.

Foldering and Boxing Documents

The following provides basic guidelines for materials' care as you re-folder and box documents for their permanent keeping. See the chapter on preservation for more specific information and for discussions of the terms used here.

- Use appropriate materials, including folders, boxes, and other materials described in the chapter on preservation, to house collections safely.
- Use upright boxes for standard collections so that materials are easily accessible.
- Use properly sized acid-/lignin-free boxes so folders do not slide.
- Boxes should be filled so folders are vertical, not slumping, but they should not be so full that folders are hard to retrieve. If boxes are not full enough, use spacers and dividers to keep folders vertical, or stuff acid-free paper in the back of the box.
- If the entire series is composed of letter-sized paper, use letter-sized folders. Otherwise, use legal-sized folders.
- When needed, score lines in the archives folders should be creased so that documents are resting flat on the bottom of the folder and do not slump.
- Store oversized flat folders in appropriately sized boxes or map drawers.
- Use pencil instead of pen to label folders. Stray pencil marks can be erased.
- Record information about the collection while processing it to use later in a finding aid.

Figure 13 This image shows upright boxes and flat boxes used for varying types of records as described later in the chapter on Preservation

Active Versus Inactive Files

Records Management

Storing expired records in your home takes up a lot of space that can better serve you in other ways. It can also cost you a lot of time and frustration to look through unnecessary materials to find what you need. So why keep "dead records" with apparently no informational value around?

Know what you use and what you are required to keep by law. (For example, short-term financial records only need retention for three to ten years.) Devise a filing system that encourages you to periodically clean out your active files. You may perhaps keep files in chronological order, and each year on the same date, remove an earlier year's worth of records that are no longer needed. You might use the end of the year or tax season as a marker. Move temporary records to a place where you can easily access them and discard them when their useful life has ended. Move materials you will retain forever in neat archival boxes. Maintain a simple index of your files to enhance your system. Treat your records as an asset and manage them efficiently.

As discussed in the previous section, the arrangement you choose for your personal files should make sense to you. It should be practical, allowing you to retrieve the items you need in a timely fashion. It should also distinguish between "active" and "inactive" records and should allow you to easily retrieve both your new and old materials.

It is generally beneficial to consider your files as two separate entities. Keep those you actively use separate from your "historical" records that are no longer used on a daily basis and are referred to only occasionally. Most of us keep active files in filing cabinets or on top of our desk in an organizer or in our desk. Inactive files that you want to keep permanently should be moved to preservation safe boxes that help ensure their longevity. The organizational separation of active files from inactive files also helps you better handle materials and makes it easier to find the records needed daily. In institutional collections that document an organization's activities, active records are retained in offices; semi-active records (the ones we need to keep temporarily) can be moved to short-term storage; and archives are moved to a separate permanent facility. This separation and the records management involved in maintaining the separation helps retain organization, making clear the purpose of records and enhancing accessibility.

Preferably, you will know the future value of your documents as you create them. Consider if the document you write or use is valuable for the short term or if it should be kept for posterity. Professionals who handle records keep a "retention schedule" that helps them move items for discarding to cheaper storage space or to permanent storage when the time comes. You can set up a similar system to transfer files when your active records become inactive. Use paper or create a database to help with this task. Note dates when items can be discarded or moved to more permanent storage out of the file cabinet or desk. Alternately, use a packaged software product for records management such as Paper Tiger.[29]

I keep a stack of papers in a bin next to my desk. These include research notes, news clippings, my daughter's most recent school papers, and other materials that come in on a regular basis. Each month, I file bills in my desk and other materials appropriately. Every year I go through the files in my desk to get rid of outdated materials, which I discard or move to archival boxes in my office closet and shelving I have arranged for this purpose. Keeping things centralized makes them accessible, making it easy for me to add materials to the collection and to use the information when I need it.

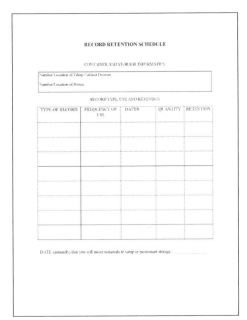

Figure 14. You may want to review your records and consider using a paper form or a software product to keep track of them. Record the types of materials you have, where they are located, how often you use them, what dates they encompass, how much space they take up, and when you should move them to set "temporary" or "permanent" storage. Decide when you will review your records annually and stick to your schedule. The end or beginning of the year is a good time to incorporate this into your life so that you remember and make sure it gets done.

---

[29] See more about Paper Tiger (www.thepapertiger.com) in the section on finding aids.

Managing Paper Records

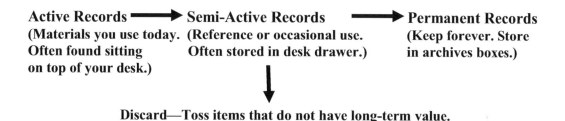

Active Records ⟶ **Semi-Active Records** ⟶ **Permanent Records**
(Materials you use today.   (Reference or occasional use.   (Keep forever. Store
Often found sitting   Often stored in desk drawer.)   in archives boxes.)
on top of your desk.)

Discard—Toss items that do not have long-term value.

Managing Computer Records

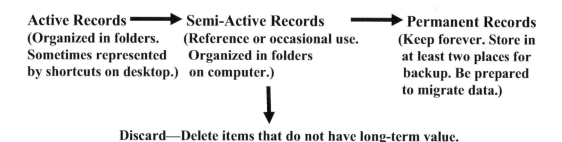

Active Records ⟶ **Semi-Active Records** ⟶ **Permanent Records**
(Organized in folders.   (Reference or occasional use.   (Keep forever. Store in
Sometimes represented   Organized in folders   at least two places for
by shortcuts on desktop.) on computer.)   backup. Be prepared
                                              to migrate data.)

Discard—Delete items that do not have long-term value.

Balancing Digital and Printed Files

Digital and printed files can be thought of as parts of one collection that are maintained separately but linked by a common origin. For example, suppose you are preparing for the holidays. You create lists on your computer of people to whom you will give presents. You create a list of the people to whom you will give Christmas cards. You have the holiday picture of the kids taken by a professional photographer, and you order the cards into which you will slip the image. You handwrite a menu for Christmas dinner. You take your own photos of holiday festivities and place them online for your family to see. Be sure to organize all of the documentation you have created together to best reflect your life story. A box of holiday memories can safely store your photos, sample cards, and handwritten list. A backup disk of your digital files might be retained within the box. Another copy can be placed on another computer as a more secure digital backup. You can also create a list that describes the contents of the box and refers people to the original digital files stored on your computer that relate to the event.

However you organize, devise a system that makes sense and easily reminds you how to continue to organize your items when you add to a collection in the future. Your scheme

Figure 15. I used these family photos to create a holiday card. Some of them were scanned from original prints; others are more recent copies from digital originals.

should be simple enough to make you want to keep up with it. Your organizational system should be one that you can easily explain to others, which ensures that you will also understand it when you return to it a few years down the road after not viewing the files for a lengthy period. Do not choose to keep a hard copy for some things and digital files for others without any reason. For example, you may keep photos in their original form, choose to make prints of all digital files, or make prints of just your favorites, but make sure whatever you do is done consistently. Also make sure that you connect the digital and print files intellectually in some way, through a printed index or database.

Let me return to some of my own files to describe how they are arranged so that you have a concrete example of a system. My nonactive business papers are arranged in archival boxes by client so I can easily pull out records related to a particular project when I need to review. I have many of my client files on a computer; these I keep on two backup hard drives as well. Because these materials are especially significant—vital to my business and used often—I keep a hard copy of my reports as further protection against computer failure and for easy retrieval. The printed collection also includes any background information my clients gave me or other research materials that I picked up to conduct my project. Digital photos from my projects are generally kept solely in computerized form in two or three copies, backed up in different formats and kept in different places. On my computer, I have a folder for each project and a separate folder labeled "Consulting Photos" with subfolders for each project. I use and reuse photos for presentations and writing purposes, so I find it useful to separate them out from the projects themselves.

For my personal papers, my old printed photographs are arranged in boxes by people within them and then by event if the event was significant enough. I have series of photos for my family and friends. Within the family grouping are photos from my childhood, teenage years, college, etc; my friend photos are arranged the same way. I find it easier to arrange my family and friends by date or occasion rather than by individual person because oftentimes a photo may include more than one subject.

My new photos are just about totally digital. I print out few. I have thousands of images of my child, whose grandparents live far away and want images of all aspects of her life so they can be a part of it. Every few months, I back up my digital photos to a secondary hard drive and to DVD. They are all organized by month. I try to "tag" photos using special software that helps me intellectually control images (though I admittedly do not keep up with this very well). Additionally, I maintain my favorite images on an online photo-sharing site for my parents to see. This also makes it easy for me to relive my favorite moments.

My most favored of these favorite images are printed and placed into archival photo albums, so we can easily browse and remember these special times. This also keeps costs down because it is expensive to put everything in good albums. (Who really wants to look at every photo you own in one sitting, anyway? And how many are really worth showing to others?) I keep albums arranged chronologically to keep the order of my life so the albums read as a kind of story about myself. I selectively choose the ones that make me happiest. I try to label printed images so I always remember who is pictured in them.

Figure 16. Much to my husband's amusement, I really do keep my personal papers arranged in archival boxes. They keep things tidy and safe. Boxes are great protection, even when other conditions for preservation are not ideal.

My school records (hard copy files) are arranged by year, and my memorabilia are kept together in their own separate box with separate folders based on the occasion. I keep my daughter's materials separate from mine and arranged similarly. This probably includes more materials than my mother ever kept when I was seven, but I am still selective and carefully have to explain to my little one why some things end up in the recycling bin. I have a separate box for artwork arranged by date. Things such as baby shoes and the little cardboard books that my daughter loved to chew as a baby are kept in a separate memorabilia box. I know some people scan everything that their kids do, but it is better to use your knowledge of appraisal to cull that which best reveals your life story or that of your loved ones. Keep the most enlightening information. Get rid of the mundane and repetitive to highlight what is valuable. It makes your story stronger, getting rid of the clutter in favor of a focused and valuable informational resource. I maintain only active and semi-active papers in nonarchival filing cabinets or boxes. When I know that I want to keep something forever, I transfer it to archival folders and an archival box. I keep a supply on hand just in case.[30]

---

[30] See the preservation section for a list of other useful archives tools to keep on hand.

Scanning

Some people like to scan old photos and documents so everything is digital. This has the benefit of keeping everything in a similar format and allows you to use one means to access it all. I recommend using digital for access and storing away the original for safekeeping, if this is feasible. Sometimes creating a scanned copy means that you can discard an original, creating more room in your home or storage space for other things, but scanning is not considered a replacement for the actual item for archives.

Sometimes the format of items enhances their value. For example, being able to touch an original diary and easily read marginalia that a digital copy might not re-create well can be beneficial. It is nice to have the original to go back to in order to verify something that is not completely clear on the scan and to serve as "evidence" of the event that lead to the document's creation. The original also sometimes possesses a sentimental value that is lost in digitization.

Keeping all of this in mind, the one drawback to scanning is that it is time-consuming. First, you must carefully think through a scanning project to avoid losing valuable information in your copies. You must have a good scanner that can create legible documents. It is useful to use a software program that helps you keep track of your materials. Scan at a high resolution to pick up details. Review the quality of the scans as you go to make sure they are legible. Organize your records before scanning so they are logical and neat. Be prepared to add useful "metadata" that provides information that allows you to easily retrieve a record from a database.

As with many ideas about keeping personal papers, there is no "one size fits all" solution. If you are more comfortable keeping information on a computer and prefer looking through digital files rather than originals, by all means scan them. Keep originals when they offer something unique that cannot be duplicated electronically. If you are not a "computer person," there is no need to scan your paper records. Think of all your materials as one collection maintained in different formats.

I scan information I wish to share. I have photos and documents from my grandparents that I use in presentations. I scan old photos to send to friends because it is easier than making them new prints. As a general rule of thumb for your cherished personal archives, view scanning as a tool for accessibility rather than as a replacement for the original. [31]

<hr/>

[31] Records kept for administrative or legal purposes may be scanned with originals discarded following certain guidelines. See "IRS Publication 552: Record Keeping for Individuals" (www.irs.gov/pub/irs-pdf/p552.pdf) for guidance on keeping tax-related information.

Organizing from the Perspective of a Librarian or Curator

The organization of books and artifacts differs from personal papers. While we aim to consider our personal papers in groups, professionals consider books and artifacts by item. Librarians generally (not always) catalog one book at a time. Curators generally (not always) care for one artifact at a time.

The two best-known standards for book organization were established by the Library of Congress (LC) and by Melvil Dewey. LC is most often used by academic libraries, and the Dewey Decimal System is found in public libraries. LC and Dewey apply numbers to represent subjects, so individual titles may be placed in a logical sequence on shelves. Today the possibilities for intellectual rearrangement of individual items are endless, with databases that can search for individual words in records that include information about title, author, subject, publisher, and more.

Objects in a museum are also considered item by item and, in a history museum, by how the artifact is used. History museums generally base their organizational scheme on a system called *nomenclature* that provides a predetermined list of terms for one to describe each item (e.g., hat, kettle, telephone). Like the Dewey Decimal System and LC, nomenclature guides the organizer by offering a specific system to make the control of objects and the information they embody easier to handle. A catalogue for collections includes information about each object, such as its accession number (when it was officially accepted into the repository's collection), material, date, maker, provenance, shelf location, and description.

The system a history museum uses is much like that we use in our home. We keep our silverware together in the kitchen. Our shoes are organized in our closet and may even be broken up by type, with high heels on one end and sneakers on the other. I even keep my personal "collections" together (like the example of my carnival glass dishes mentioned on page 20).

The systems used by cultural heritage institutions have been adapted because of their determined suitability for our needs over time. They are logical when considering diverse items. Adapt the strategies, using the wisdom and classification fine-tuning of professionals, but do not be afraid to step outside of the box when you need to for your own personal things. Standards should make life easier, make items easier to find, and help you think about collections in logical ways. They should not be a burden to you.

Mental and Writing Exercises for Organizing Archives

1. Review your documentation and determine how many "collections" you have. Consider who created the materials. Were they all created by you, or were some passed down through generations?

2. Look at the collection(s) in your possession and determine whether there is any order to the records. Is it chronological or alphabetical, or is there some other imposed scheme?

3. If there is no order to your collections, glance through the materials and identify dominant groupings. Can you organize things by subject, by person, or chronologically? For each dominant group you identify, list smaller groupings into which materials can be broken.

4. After thinking about organization, look for strengths in your collections. Are there any subjects or dates for which there is a lot of information? Is there any especially interesting information or information that highlights a particularly noteworthy aspect of your life or society?

5. Look for weaknesses in your collections. Are there any subjects or dates missing from your materials? Are there especially noteworthy aspects of your life that are not represented in your materials?

6. Determine which of the materials in your possession are "active." Do any of them have long-term value? Will you discard others after some time?

7. Where do your digital and print files overlap? Which of your materials are only available in print? Which are only digital?

Chapter Four:
Describing Information

Purpose of Finding Aids

- To help you locate materials
- To help you understand the context of materials
- To provide biographical information about the creator of the materials
- To provide information about the depth and breadth of a collection
- To describe the arrangement of materials
- To highlight enlightening or important elements of a collection
- To describe relationships between separate groups of materials
- To note similar materials in other places
- For a repository, to provide administrative information such as copyright restrictions and rules for use

Archives Finding Aids

Creating "finding aids" and trying your hand at describing family materials helps you create a more meaningful collection to pass on to loved ones. As I discussed in the last chapter, while arranging material and handling individual documents, consider how all the papers fit together and what kind of community information they provide. Finding aids allow you to put your conclusions in writing and to document the connections you have identified between materials. They serve as a sort of index to archives. (You can think "index" when I say "finding aid" if that is easier for now.) Finding aids are not a necessary part of a home collection, but they can serve as useful tools for you and for future generations.

For example, consider two folders of correspondence. One is labeled "Katie." One is labeled "Diane." Suppose that these folders were passed down to you from family members and you have no idea who Katie and Diane are. As you sort through files, you learn that Katie and Diane were sisters. You learn when they were born, where they lived, and what their maiden and married names were. You learn that they wrote to each other once a week; the correspondence you have shows their back-and-forth conversations. Both of their husbands served in the Civil War, and their correspondence discusses how they coped during those tumultuous years. You even learn that Katie and Diane were your great-great-great aunts. These connections you have made between Katie, Diane, and yourself can be documented in a finding aid so future viewers of the collection do not need to put the pieces together as you have done.

Finding aids also allow you to create alternate arrangements for materials. Most family-based collections rely on simple systems of organization that include chronologically or alphabetically arranged files. The finding aid gives additional "access points" into one's documentation and facilitates the records' use. For example, say you have a series of correspondence files organized by date, but you think it would be useful to alphabetize the collection by correspondent. Create a finding aid that lists correspondents alphabetically and then cite the folders in which their letters appear.

Creating finding aids for family materials can increase a collection's usefulness. Collections are most functional for research purposes, and specific materials within it are easiest to access when there is a tool describing the collection's contents. While our organizational efforts in the previous chapter focused on making it easy for us to use materials, our description of materials has the added value of making it easy for anyone to understand them and place them in context.[32] In fact, finding aids created by individuals for their personal papers are a boon to archivists if papers are donated to a repository. They can help the archivist better understand family history and collection context. The access tools you create will be examined and integrated into any finding aids the Archives writes for materials you donate.

Finding aids in the home collection are most useful for describing collections that are near completion. If you are continually adding new materials to a record group you called "correspondence," for example, you will continually be updating your finding aids. It may not be appropriate to create a finding aid for them yet. Consider creating finding aids for materials that have been passed down to you or for groups of records that are a closed set, as in those files to which you think you will be adding no more material. Whether passing your materials onto loved ones or donating them to a repository, treat your finding aid as a valuable part of your collection of family papers. A printed finding aid can be placed at the front of a collection, but a copy should also be kept separately with administrative files. In your home, you may want to keep this in a file cabinet stored with insurance records and a list of household items. Alternately, you can create a digital file, as in a word processing document or database that describes your materials. Keep backup copies in your home and off-site.

---

[32] This chapter focuses on the "descriptive inventory," which is a specific type of finding aid that is most useful for describing personal papers. I use the term "finding aid" to avoid confusion, but please be aware that archival repositories apply this term to more tools than I describe here.

Asking Questions

I corresponded with Elenita Chickering as I processed her collection at the Gardner Museum. I asked questions about her work and the organization of her materials. Below is part of her response to my inquiry in July 2004. It reflects how, perhaps similar to all of us, Ms. Chickering did not at first fully realize the value of her own collections. Her letter was informative and is a valuable addition toward helping us understand the resource she created.

Dear Ms. Mannon,
Thank you for your letter and questions. Without wishing to be excessively modest, I confess to being embarrassed by the Gardner Museum's even wanting my voluminous research on Arthur Stone. I began this monograph many years ago, simply wishing to record a few details for my own family so they would have an idea of Stone's accomplishments and wouldn't just casually ignore his stature as silversmith…. As for my rather voluminous correspondence…I organized most of it for my own convenience, often in haste, and mostly alphabetical by correspondent's name or by an arbitrary heading for easy access on my part….

A finding aid will help those who need to care for your collection when you no longer care for it. It will help them to recognize the value of your personal archives, to maintain them as you desire, and to access historical information about your family. You can use any list you create now to help determine what materials are missing from your life story. It may encourage you to create more documentation in those areas to better care for your family history.

The end of this chapter includes two model finding aids—one for the collection of Elizabeth Robbins Berry of Carlisle, Massachusetts, and one for the collection of Elenita Chickering of Gardner, Massachusetts. Pay particular attention to the box and folder lists found in these examples. These lists are usually the main components of the finding aid. The box and folder list can be accompanied by the more descriptive pieces highlighted in the rest of this chapter, some of which are also included in our models. The most common descriptive pieces are the scope and content note, which fits materials into context, and the biographical note, which provides background information about the subject or creator of the records. These elements add information you garnered during your arrangement of the collection, picked up from additional research, or learned from people associated with the collection itself. I have created genealogy trees, researched and noted specialized terms, and created indices referencing important people or events I have found among collections of personal papers.

Creating a finding aid is one of my favorite things to do. It can be quite simple or can be complex, allowing you to use your creativity to design new structures to your collections so that they are easier to understand and so that information is easier to locate. Creating a finding aid can also open doors for identifying new information that you may not have previously considered or understood.

Elements of a Finding Aid

- **Abstract**—Provides basic information about a collection. Often serves as a cover page for the finding aid. It includes:
    o Title of collection and/or collection creator
    o Dates of materials contained within
    o Volume of records (usually given in number of boxes or linear feet)
    o Location of records (where in your home you keep them)
    o Provenance (Who made the records and who owned them? Have they been passed down to you by family members?)
    o Name of person who processed collection and date of processing (this will be you if you are the person who organized and preserved the collection and if you are creating the finding aid)

- **Scope and content note**—Explains what the records tell us. Includes such information as what people are included in the collection, what time periods and special events are covered, and how this collection relates to events in a larger historical contest.

- **Biographical note**—Gives information about the person(s) to whom the collection relates.

- **Arrangement note**—Describes the organization of materials.

- **Series list and/or description**—Details your groupings of the material.

- **Box and folder list**—Lists boxes and folders.

- **Specialized indices or research tools (optional access tools)**—Genealogies, timelines, etc.

Preparing for Collection Description

In the last chapter, I wrote about how one should take notes while physically arranging a collection. I wrote about how, during this process, one should try to gain a broad view of materials. Write down anything you learn that makes the collection more interesting and understandable. Seek to identify elements of the collection that may not be immediately apparent to others who may look through it. For example, you may figure out that one person is related to another or that a family was involved in an important larger historical event. This information will prove useful for later, more comprehensive, description. As you process your family papers, you will make connections and realizations about the materials that may not be visible to the casual observer. As you organize and gain a broad perspective of the collection, take notes about its smaller pieces.

Archivists use finding aids to express these elements, pointing out connections among material while aiming to provide a better understanding of the

Reconstituting a Life

Organizing and describing a collection amounts to reconstructing the past. One must try to represent life events as accurately as possible, highlighting what is important through proper arrangement and description. When focusing on the elements of a finding aid, one must become a bit of a biographer, taking a look at the person whose collection is before them and evaluating that person's life. Whether you are describing your own life or that of a family member, the act of gathering a synopsis of one's personal history allows you to be a little creative. Use your imagination to relay the interesting facts about a person and to help re-create a personality. Who were the important people in the person's life? What were the important events? Why would anyone want to know about this person? What unusual things happened to him? What everyday things that happened to him show his life in an historical context? The collection you process becomes a little bit your own when you work on it, even if you did not create the materials before you. I feel as if I am a friend or an acquaintance of every person whose collection I have processed, even those long gone. Processing collections for me is as good as reading a well-crafted novel.

individual(s) who created the papers. Consider what is most interesting among your materials and what information may be most desirable to access in the future. If the physical arrangement of your items does not make these elements obvious, consider creating a finding aid that will help.[33] The finding aid can describe the collection as a whole or can explore the various levels of arrangement you created. Your level of description can list boxes of materials, describe series, or list folders.

Item-level description is rarely created. It is time-consuming, and if you

Complex Collections

Among the most interesting materials I have processed are the papers of the MacKaye Family Collection belonging to the Shirley Historical Society in Massachusetts. (The MacKayes were a famous theater family, but to a modern audience, the best-known member of the family was Benton MacKaye, who developed the idea for the Appalachian Trail.) The collection includes a little bit about various members of the family. I organized it by person, creating a series for each and then subseries such as "correspondence" and "plays." In the finding aid, I included short biographical pieces for individuals and created a genealogy chart to show their relationships. The society owns quite a few books written by and about the MacKayes, so I create a list of these. I also included a "correspondent name index" that lists who wrote to each family member. Dartmouth College has more materials by and about the MacKayes. I wrote to them to get a copy of their finding aid so researchers could see both when exploring the Shirley collection. It was expected that this collection would get a lot of use. So, the more information we could give about its contents, the more useful it would be to researchers looking for particular information. Additionally, the documents would be safer from destruction as they now require less handling by people seeking specific information. Such handling can be a preservation concern—thus, this work contributes to the longevity of materials.

---

[33] Archives repositories have additional types of finding aids in their arsenal that are not discussed in detail here. One type, for example, is the accession register, where the institution records what materials are added to the collection, who donated them, and when. If you are interested in learning more about the basics of archives to inform your personal or related professional interest, or if you are a family historian looking to better understand our methods to help your research, please see the bookstore at the Society of American Archivists website (www2.archivists.org) for more information.

did your arrangement work with some thought, it is unnecessary. Items grouped together because of their similarities to each other and their ability to reveal a context together should be described together.

When you are comfortable with your understanding of your materials, write a basic description of the contents of your collection. Prepare to add more details over time. The following sections describe details of specific elements that can be included in your finding aid. A general description of the collection can be followed by lists of series, folder titles, and descriptions of a collection's parts.

Formatting for Dates

Recorded dates can provide us and those who look at records in the future with valuable information. Include dates in the abstract of the finding aid, on each box label, and on the right side of each folder.

- If records are not dated, write "ND"
- For inclusive dates, write dates separated by a dash: 2009–2010
- For a collection where the bulk of the material takes up just a few years, write the dates with dashes, with the bulk in parentheses: (1990 – (1999–2002) – 2010)
- For a collection missing a few years, use two dashes: (1980 – – 2010)

Missing dates make me wonder about lost materials and sometimes set me on a mission to find them. Other times, missing dates clue me in that a person's life differed at that time. The person may not have been as actively recording information. Perhaps they were away or going through a major life event that precluded them from documenting. Or, maybe, an individual destroyed specific documentation that he did not want to remember and did not want others to see, such as love letters from a past boyfriend or pictures from those awkward high school years.

Introduction

Create a cover page for your description that lists the title of the collection. The title should be straightforward and should convey the creator of the materials. For example, if the materials were written by me, I would call the group of records "Melissa Mannon Collection." If you are caring for materials that were created by someone else—perhaps they were passed down to you—write the name of the person who created the files. It would say something such as "Joe Jones Collection." If the documents were created by more than one person, give them an inclusive title such as "Jones Family Papers." Or, if the family has more than one name, you could include more than one and write something such as "Jones and Smith Family Papers."

The Melissa Mannon Collection
1980 – 2010

Processed by: Melissa Mannon, May 2011

15 document boxes

Alongside the title, record the inclusive dates of materials in the collection. Explain if anyone owned or cared for these materials before they came into your possession. Include the name of the person who organized the collection and the date of organization in this introductory piece.

Describing Included Information

A "scope and content note" includes a summary of what is contained in a collection, its depth and breadth, its strengths, and its weaknesses. The scope and content note provides a broad overview of materials, while also noting a collection's highlights and unique contents. The scope and content note allows the collection processor to be creative. This does not mean you will invent information, but it provides an opportunity for you to make intellectual connections between materials. It describes how documents in a collection relate to each other. The note also places the documentation in a larger context, explaining how the creator of the documents developed and used information. The processor of a collection may do research to better understand the materials and can use that knowledge to create a more useful finding aid that discusses how the materials fit into a larger social history.

Information that you know or think you know can be used to make the finding aid even more useful. If you have heard stories from others that shed light on materials, try to write it down. Make sure that you indicate where you got your information. For example make a note such as: "These materials were passed down from Aunt Sally, who got them from Great-Uncle Bill. She told me that he stored the records in his attic and would take time to talk to his kids about their family history and show them these materials while they all sat around a candle lamp." Make sure you note your name as the person passing on this information and the date you recorded it. Keep in mind that this information may or may not be true if there is no evidence to back it up.[34]

Scope and Content Sample

The text below is a portion of the short scope and content note from the Albert Ryan collection at the Waltham Public Library in Massachusetts. This note provides a brief overview of what one will find in the collection. More detailed scope and content notes are given as models at the end of this chapter, but this one is an example of the bare-bones basics. It was written when time was pressing to complete the processing of other collections in the Archives:

This collection contains the personal papers of the Ryan family. The Ryans are a well-known family in Waltham History. Housed here are: Papers of Albert M. Ryan I, who was a Waltham historian in the late nineteenth century; Papers of his brother, Samuel Lyman Ryan, who served in the Civil War; Correspondence of the brothers' father, Henry M. Ryan I, who was one of the Forty-niners; materials relating to Ida Annah Ryan, daughter of Albert M. Ryan I and a famous female architect at the turn of the twentieth century; Papers of Albert M. Ryan II and Henry Ryan II, grandsons of Albert M. Ryan I. Other family related materials in this collection include family genealogy with information pertaining to the Ryans, the Whitneys, the Jameson family, the Barneses, and the Law family. Family photos are also housed here and include views of Chapel Hill, the Ryan family farm, Old Prospect Barn, the Waltham Depot train wreck, Fox Island, Ryan family portraits, and other views of Waltham.

---

[34] See the sample collection examples in the following chapters in this book for models of scope and content and other elements of descriptive inventories.

Biography

Who's That Girl?

The biographical note of Elizabeth Robbins Berry at the end of this chapter is a good sample from a finding aid. For your personal papers, provide a comprehensive overview of your life or your family. You do not need to have exceptional writing skills to do this. Your biographical note may take the form of a simple bulleted list or timeline that spells out important events in your life, highlights important people, and notes the things that you consider to be formative to your development. Be creative and make it fun. It is fascinating to consider what should be recorded about a person.

Using information found within the collection or performing research to better understand the people mentioned in a collection can help a processor better explain the value of materials to an outsider. The creation of a "biographical note" allows a collection caretaker to record basic information about the creators and previous owners of the collection, while describing their lives in a cultural context. Explain how those mentioned in the collection reflect a particular time and place and how their activities reflect those of their communities and society.

The biographical note should contain confirmed information about the creator of the collection. It may also be useful to record additional information about others mentioned in the collection if they are noteworthy or contributed to the collection in some significant way. Biographical information can be gleaned from the records themselves or gathered from independent research. It is useful for you to rely a bit on your personal knowledge of family and the materials on hand to create guides to your collections. However, do not present your thoughts and suppositions as fact. Note how you came to your conclusions and reveal your opinions. When information is gathered from research, record the resources from which it came.

Recording biographical information can be helpful in determining or evaluating the provenance of a collection. Recording from where the materials came and the relationship of the person who handed the collection to you speaks to the authenticity of the items. You may want to note something such as: "These materials were passed down to me, Melissa Mannon, from Aunt Sally, who was married to Uncle Bill. Bill is the son of Jeremiah, who is the author of these records." Or, if the history of ownership is somewhat cloudy, note that the information came from your personal knowledge or family legend, but that it is not backed by the primary papers in the collection or by firsthand knowledge.

In certain cases, I have found it useful to create family trees for collections in repositories so I could ensure that I understood the relationships of those mentioned in the records. Consider what aids you can create to make the context of the records clearer. Feel free to add elements that will explain the materials to others.

Figure 18. If this photograph were part of a larger collection, a biographical note would give us the background story so we could better understand the context in which the image was taken.

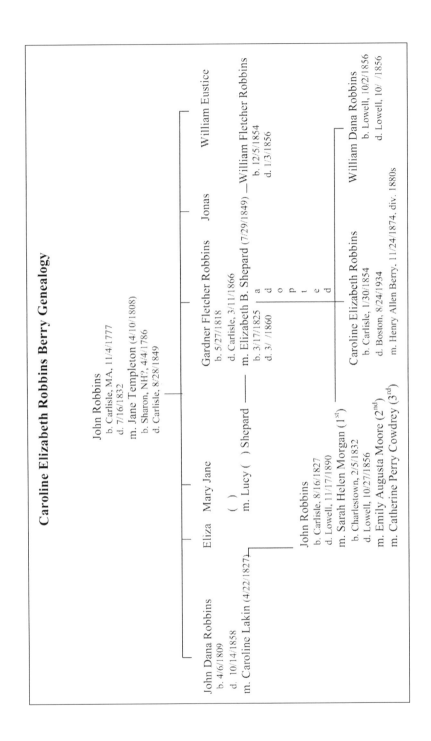

Caroline Elizabeth Robbins Berry Genealogy

John Robbins
    b. Carlisle, MA, 11/4/1777
    d. 7/16/1832
    m. Jane Templeton (4/10/1808)
        b. Sharon, NH?, 4/4/1786
        d. Carlisle, 8/28/1849

William Eustice

Jonas

Gardner Fletcher Robbins
    b. 5/27/1818
    d. Carlisle, 3/11/1866
    m. Elizabeth B. Shepard (7/29/1849) — William Fletcher Robbins
        b. 3/17/1825   b. 12/5/1854
        d. 3/ /1860   d. 1/3/1856
        a
        d
        o
        p
        t
        e
        d

William Dana Robbins
    b. Lowell, 10/2/1856
    d. Lowell, 10/ /1856

Caroline Elizabeth Robbins
    b. Carlisle, 1/30/1854
    d. Boston, 8/24/1934
    m. Henry Allen Berry. 11/24/1874. div. 1880s

Eliza Mary Jane

( )
m. Lucy ( ) Shepard

John Robbins
    b. Carlisle, 8/16/1827
    d. Lowell, 11/17/1890
    m. Sarah Helen Morgan (1st)
        b. Charlestown, 2/5/1832
        d. Lowell, 10/27/1856
    m. Emily Augusta Moore (2nd)
    m. Catherine Perry Cowdrey (3rd)

John Dana Robbins
    b. 4/6/1809
    d. 10/14/1858
    m. Caroline Lakin (4/22/1827)

Describing Organization

An "arrangement note" describes how material within a collection is organized. It tells if it is alphabetical, ordered by date, or if someone has applied some other scheme to categorize materials. It discusses who applied this arrangement—if the collection was organized this way by its creator or the person who processed the materials. It discusses in what condition the materials were first found by the processor, if he rearranged some of the collection, and why. The note discusses how the arrangement aids access to the collection and if an alternate arrangement would provide different values for accessibility.

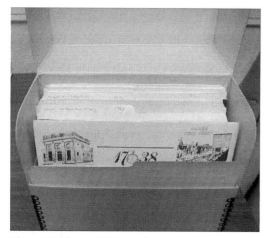

Figure 19. Show off the neat arrangement of your work by describing what you have done in an arrangement note.

Arrangement Note

This short arrangement note clearly identifies who organized the materials and how. Within the sample collection are published materials that are housed separately; their differing arrangement is noted. Arrangement notes can be long and complicated or short and sweet, depending on what was done to the collection they describe.

"Archival series were artificially created by the consulting archivist. Materials are arranged by record type. Within each grouping, materials are organized chronologically.

"Research materials are arranged and identified using standard bibliographic format, are organized by type, and are arranged chronologically within each folder."

From the collection of the Massachusetts Moderator's Association. Carlisle, MA.

Series Descriptions

I created series descriptions for the Elenita Chickering collection finding aid, which is located at the end of this chapter. Chickering created her own groupings of records. As I processed the collection, I picked up clues about her thinking. Series 1, duplicated below, provides a good example of series description:

Series 1—Plans for Publication

The first series relates to plans for publication and was originally located in ten loose-leaf notebooks. Chickering referred to these records as "monograph material." The group includes the following subseries: "Front Matter, Text and Notes"; "Monograph"; "Domestic Hollowware 1901–07, 1908–13, 1919–20, 1925–37"; "Illustration Captions"; and "End Matter." Within this series can be found photographs of artwork, Stone family photographs, photograph captions, correspondence (including primarily permissions to reproduce photographs), and notes regarding plans for Chickering's book.

Describing Groups

One creates a "series description" when one feels that an accounting of multiple folders will be helpful toward understanding a collection's contents. It is not always included in the finding aid. This description provides the scope of each series, similar to a scope note, but is aimed at small groupings of material. It reflects the reason for a particular arrangement of materials and the value of these materials in a larger context. In this section of the finding aid, you have flexibility to describe the relationship between larger sets of papers (series) and smaller ones (subseries) within the collection. Aim to reflect the divisions in the collection that help one understand the amount of material related to a topic. Aim to highlight the importance of smaller collection sets to facilitate one's understanding of the collection as a whole. Create a series description when there are outstanding separations between items, when these materials can use more detailed explanation, when you have intimate knowledge about the series that you want to share, or when you just feel that the other elements of the finding aid do not adequately describe the subsets of materials.

Box and Folder List

A "box and folder list" is exactly what you probably think it is: It is simply the recording of the titles of boxes and folders in your collection. In the previous section of this book, you were taught how to write titles on your folders. Transcribe those folder titles into your box and folder list. Be sure to record the number of boxes and the number of folders for each similar grouping of records. For example, record four boxes of correspondence as "Correspondence (4 boxes)." For a series of four folders of correspondence from your mom, write "Correspondence, Mom [plus her full name] (4 folders)." Include dates using the format provided earlier. The box and folder list is one of the basic components of a collection's finding aid and is almost always included to enhance access.

The Magic of Finding Aids

As a case in point, let us suppose that I was arranging the records of a prominent artist. That artist kept correspondence files, copies of invoices of his sales, and notebooks of sketches. Among his correspondence files were personal letters written by a gentleman whom the artist had met at an art gallery opening. Those letters were written on personal letterhead and included information about the private lives of the men, such as tales about their children's exploits and vacations. Let us also suppose that this friend of the artist was also the director of a famous museum. The museum bought a painting from the artist and the director thanked the artist and complimented his work using official museum letterhead. Other museum workers also wrote to the artist to set a price for the piece and to determine delivery particulars and other official matter. There was an invoice for the transactions, and there was a draft copy of the work still among the artist's sketch files. We would find all of this information spread throughout the collection. The director would be represented in the series of private correspondence; he would also be found among correspondence from the museum. A link to the museum would also be found in the artist's financials, and there is a connection to the artwork the museum owns in the series of sketches. We can point out these connections within our finding aids, making access easier and creating additional research value.

Optional Access Tools

Some common indices that are helpful for home collections include:

Genealogy or family tree—Helps individuals understand the relationship of record creators to others, especially other individuals who may be included in the collections

Glossary of terms—Definitions of words or personal jargon that appear in the collection and may not be obvious to everyone

Keys—Provide information about specialized coding that one may have applied in the organization of the collection; include things such as color codes or abbreviations

List of names—Includes people, places, or important things that appear scattered throughout the collection and are not evident in the folder structure and descriptions of the collection

Register of correspondence—Listing of who sent letters to whom and when

Timeline—Lists important events related specifically to collections or parallels larger historical events with those in the

Additional Access Tools

The basic manuscript inventory, upon which we have focused in this chapter, is just one type of finding aid. Indices to specific portions of the collection are also useful for inclusion. For example, lists of correspondents with dates of their letters are commonly found in finding aids. The collection processor may create lists of well-known people found in a collection or may highlight particularly relevant events and places. Lists of unusual words, jargon relevant to the collection, keys to acronyms, and other collection-specific terms might also be included. Illustrative tools such as family trees can also have a place in explaining and providing better access to materials.

Computerized Findings Aids

Computerized databases for managing archives are becoming more common. They can be a useful tool for managing personal papers in the home. Although many people will not have the inclination to describe all of the materials we own in a database, we may desire to get better access to particular materials. A database is advantageous for its use of searching terms (metadata) to make it easy to get at specific bits of information in a collection. It is also useful when you want to continue to add information and description to a growing collection.

Professionally, archivists have created sweeping standardized systems for capturing information about collections and providing access to that information.[35] These descriptive tools are beyond the scope of this book. However, user-friendly, smaller systems to enter information about a variety of collections can be useful to an individual with diverse collections in the home. Packaged programs for the home user can address the specific needs of personal papers. Their usefulness ranges from the organization of materials you wish to keep permanently, to the availability of disposal schedules for determining what can be discarded and when, to creating a home inventory for insurance purposes.

Elements of a Collection Database

A database that holds information about your collection can be as specific as you want to make it, considering your time constraints. The following elements are useful for helping you make your collection accessible:

- Type of documents (paper, e-mail, photos, etc.)
- Series or record group
- Location
- Individual items of importance
- Scope of collection
- Notes
- Arrangement
- Dates of materials
- Metadata

---

[35] EAD, Dublin Core, and other systems embraced by professional archivists focus on standardizing descriptive elements so all professionals can easily incorporate similar data into finding aids and make them usable on the Internet for widespread information distribution. These standards specify what information to enter and how to enter it.

There is software available for helping with personal files, both electronic and printed. This software allows you to record your files in groupings or individually, to convey the location of your materials, make notes about the materials (the scope of materials and important related information), and to apply metadata that will make it easier to locate information. Programs such as Paper Tiger allow you to manage paper files with a ready-made database.[36] Without specialized software, a computer-savvy individual can create a database with Microsoft Access or other generalized database software to suit her needs.

There are small software packages that perform specific organizational tasks for home use. ACDSee™, for example, is a well-known software package for identifying and tracking digital photographs. It allows the user to intellectually organize images by type and then enter terms for individual photos so they are easy to find. When creating computerized databases, one should stick to the same tenets as when arranging files and describing them. In general, it is not desirable to describe collections item by item. Photographs can be described as a single series. Stick with recording information about groups unless a particular item is extremely noteworthy and you want to access it quickly without searching through a folder of other items.

A database gives us a neat way to enter search terms related to a series of related images so that we can find what we need. Your database may include names of people in the images, where the images were taken, when they were taken, and other elements that would help one place images in context. When time allows, tag individual items with information as you would label individual printed images. Some programs, such as Picasa, can even "learn" to identify the faces that you have identified at least once in other photos.

There is a difference between creating a database to help you access materials and creating a database that maintains scanned copies of your materials. Many people scan materials to "preserve" them, free up space in their home, or share their information with others. In this case, your database becomes a surrogate collection rather than just a tool to access your printed files. See the chapter on digitization for more information.

---

[36] According to the Paper Tiger website (www.thepapertiger.com/tour#2), "Paper Tiger is an indexing method. It is a very simple, yet powerful concept. Keep your paper in its original form (you do not have to scan it) and use the power of the computer to quickly and easily find/share the information when you need it."

Researching Your Collections

Consider the materials you keep. Have you ever grown curious about them? From unidentified faces in photos to your mother's correspondence, from people you know nothing about to your own diary entries about forgotten events, consider digging deeper. Ask questions of those who may have information about your materials that you do not possess. Perform research to try to uncover information about things you find. Make attempts to fit tidbits about someone's life into the events of the time. An archivist often goes beyond creating a simple finding aid to creating extensive biographical or historical notes that may help researchers find what they need. For your personal archives, this type of research can be enlightening and personally fulfilling. Information can help you piece together a family tree, allow you to learn more about history, or help you feel closer to people, events, and places mentioned in your materials. Use this opportunity to explore your creativity, identify connections among personal communities, and uncover history that might otherwise be lost to time or forgotten.

Model Collection—Elizabeth Robbins Berry of Carlisle

Figure 20. Elizabeth Robbins Berry from her collection at the Carlisle Historical Society.

One of the best parts of being an archivist is the remarkable people I discover in the stacks of collections. I find that as I organize and become familiar with the records in a collection, I develop a relationship with the person reflected in it. I feel as if I know the person because I am privy to the materials (and sometimes the thoughts) that they held closest to them.

One of my most memorable personalities is Elizabeth Robbins Berry. Elizabeth had a connection to Clara Barton, who founded the Red Cross, which makes her collection interesting to those outside of her hometown of Carlisle, Massachusetts. However, Elizabeth's story is noteworthy in its own right. As a strong, divorced career woman in the nineteenth century, she lived through a transition in women's history.

Every town has well-known characters, some of whom are quite famous. In other cases, however, the people of whom we are most proud are relatively unknown outside of our communities. Elizabeth fits this profile.

I describe the collection, its parts, and my handling of it in a scope and content note and an arrangement note for the collection. The biographical note that I write includes a little bit of information I uncovered about the collection's fascinating creator. I attempt to spark others' interest in her life. Berry's collection is not the norm, in that it gave me the opportunity to arrange materials from scratch. In many cases, materials come to archives repositories with some form of arrangement that must be fine-tuned. In this case, it was up to me to determine what materials logically could be grouped together in folders as series. This is a good example for when you try to organize your own personal materials from square one.

Carlisle Historical Society
Heald Homestead
Concord Street
Carlisle, MA

Elizabeth Robbins Berry Collection

[1869 – – 1933]

Processing date: January 2002
Processed by: Melissa Mannon, Consulting Archivist

Collection size: 2 document boxes
Access: This collection is unrestricted
Copyright: Permission to publish material from this collection is subject to approval by the Carlisle Historical Society Officers
Processing: Processing of this collection was funded by a grant from the Massachusetts Historic Records Advisory Board

Scope and Content Note

The Elizabeth Robbins Berry collection includes Berry's writings, ephemera/souvenirs, photographs, and Clara Barton materials. The materials range from 1869 through 1933, with most materials not dated.

The bulk of the collection comprises the writings of Elizabeth Robbins Berry, including original handwritten manuscripts, typed manuscripts, and copies by Martha Fifield Wilkins. This series is not a complete set of Berry's writings. A noticeable gap includes her work about churches that appeared as a series in the *Republic Magazine*. (We have only #2 and #6 in the series.) The subjects of Berry's writings included in this collection are Clara Barton, the American flag, the Pledge of Allegiance, patriotism, historic American churches, Memorial Day and other holidays, historical persons and places, and Carlisle.

An important series within this collection is related to the founder of the American Red Cross and friend of Berry, Clara Barton. This series includes correspondence from Barton to Berry comprising four letters dating from 1909 to 1911. The original envelopes are included in the folder. In addition, in this series are memorial materials and news clippings related to Barton, photographs of Barton, and information about Charles Sumner Young, who was a Barton biographer. Berry's special interest in the American flag and patriotism is represented in this collection with two folders of ephemera related primarily to the flag and Francis Scott Key.

The most personal items in the collection were contained in a handmade box, which is now part of the society's artifact collection and is labeled "Lucy Shepard." The archival materials removed from the box include the oldest item found in the collection, which is a letter to Elizabeth Robbins from Gardner Fletcher Robbins. The series also includes family photographs and Berry ephemera such as her DAR membership certificate.

There are many photographs of Robbins family members in the collection. Photo albums, not housed with this material, also include images of the Robbins family.

Biographical Note

Figure 21. Elizabeth Robbins Berry as a child, from her collection at the Carlisle Historical Society

Caroline Elizabeth Robbins was born to John and Sarah Helen (Morgan) Robbins on January 30, 1854. Her mother, and brother William Dana Robbins, died a few days after the boy's birth in 1856. Soon afterwards, her grand-uncle Gardner Fletcher Robbins and his wife Elizabeth B. Shepard Robbins adopted Caroline. The couple had only one other child, a son, who died at thirteen months.

Gardner Fletcher Robbins raised Caroline Elizabeth on his own for a number of years after his wife died in 1860. During his service in the Civil War, his adopted daughter lived with his sister, Mrs. Albert Boynton.

Caroline Elizabeth Robbins married Henry Allen Berry on November 24, 1874. The couple had no children and was divorced in the early 1880s.

Best known as Elizabeth Robbins Berry, the young woman went on to serve the causes of patriotism, history, and public life through her writings and civil work.

[She was] for many years connected with the American Cultivator Publishing Company, [served] on the editorial staff of the Boston Budget, *was managing editor of the* Republic Magazine *at Washington, D.C.; [was] a successful writer of both prose and poetry, [was] well known as a club woman, being a member of the New England Press Association; past president of the Boston Proof Readers Association, Regent of the Dorchester Heights Chapter of the Daughter of the Revolution, and later of Lucia Knox Chapter; D.R. nine years in all; also president of Dahlgrin Relief Corps, No. 20, Woman's Relief Corps, also of Suffolk County*

Association head of the National Department of Patriotic Instruction and National Press Corps President.[37]

Berry was a prolific writer, who wrote under many pseudonyms, including Carolyn Robins, Elizabeth Heald, Caroline Heald, and Betty Bee. Her writings include publications for the *Republic Magazine* and the *New England Magazine.*[38]

While working in Washington, D.C., she met many prominent people, including Clara Barton, founder of the American Red Cross, with whom she became friendly.

Berry resided in Boston for most of her life. Her known residences include: 523 Newbury Street; 146 Massachusetts Avenue, Suite 432; Greenville Street, Roxbury, Massachusetts; and 625 Munsey Building.

Caroline Elizabeth Robbins Berry died on August 24, 1934, at the Home for Aged Women, Jamaica Plain, Boston. She was cremated, and the ashes were buried in the family lot in Green Cemetery, Carlisle, Massachusetts.[39]

Arrangement Note with Box and Folder List

Elizabeth Berry's personal materials are housed at the beginning of the collection, including her writings and the personal papers originally housed in the "Lucy Shepard" box. There was originally no order to Berry's writings. They have been organized by the archivist into eight series: "Clara Barton," "Memorial Day and Holidays," "Nation's Capitol," "Publications," "Historic Places," "Historic Persons," "Flags and Patriotism," and "Miscellaneous." Berry's ephemera and souvenirs are arranged at the end of the collection, with Clara Barton–related material in the middle. Clara Barton correspondence is arranged in ascending date order. Other material about the nurse is arranged by material type. Photographs are currently housed in Box 2, but they should be moved to a small box befitting their size and format.

---

[37] Wilkins Notebooks, Gleason Public Library, Carlisle, Massachusetts.
[38] Cited in *Reader's Guide to Periodical Literature*, 1904.
[39] Elizabeth Robbins Berry Collection. Carlisle Historical Society, Carlisle, Massachusetts.

Box 1

Folder 1—Elizabeth Robbins Berry—Clara Barton Lectures and Writings
Folder 2—Elizabeth Robbins Berry—Memorial Day and Holiday Writings
Folder 3—Elizabeth Robbins Berry—Nation's Capitol Writings
Folder 4—Elizabeth Robbins Berry—Publications: The Republic Magazine
Folder 5—Elizabeth Robbins Berry—Historic Places
Folder 6—Elizabeth Robbins Berry—Historic Persons
Folder 7—Elizabeth Robbins Berry—Flags and Patriotism
Folder 8—Elizabeth Robbins Berry—Miscellaneous Writings
Folder 9—Elizabeth Robbins Berry—Correspondence from Clara Barton, 1909–1911
Folder 10—Lucy Shepard Personal Papers

Box 2

Folder 1 & 2—Clara Barton Biographical
Folder 3—Clara Barton Photographs
Folder 4—Clara Barton Memoriam Booklets
Folder 5—Applications for the Clara Barton Memorial Tree, 1923
Folder 6—Charles Sumner Young (author of Clara Barton biography)

[This collection's finding aid includes an item list, which is not reflected in this model. The item list includes each document in the collection. It is unusual to include that as a tool for a collection, but this particular collection is small, the list did not take much time to create, and the project allowed for that. The repository may also use this to seek more related writings to fill gaps in Berry's papers.]

Model Collection—Elenita Chickering of Gardner

Elenita Chickering's collection came to the Gardner Museum in good order. I was hired to process the collection—to rehouse materials, ensure none of the papers were in disarray, and enhance access.

Elenita was a biographer, renowned in her own right, but not as well known as the subject of her work. The collection is valuable because it provides insight into Ms. Chickering's work, but it also is an authoritative resource for information about the artist Arthur J. Stone. I therefore had to be sensitive to highlighting both people when I worked on this collection. I considered who might use the materials—both people interested in the artist and people interested in the writer. Researchers could be interested in one or the other, or in both and their relationship.

As I did for the Berry collection, I described the collection and its parts in a scope and content note. Unlike the Berry collection, the arrangement note reflects the order given to the collection by Elenita Chickering, while describing my role during processing. Ms. Chickering created her own finding aids for the collection, and I also describe those here and discuss what role they play as access tools for collection users. To enhance the arrangement already given to the collection, I added series descriptions to discuss the contents of each series. This allowed me to identify the logic to the order the original arranger of the collection applied. I also used this section to define some terms I discovered that were probably obvious to Ms. Chickering, but that were not obvious to me and would probably not be obvious to collection users.

This section includes a sample piece from the finding aid.

Gardner Museum
Gardner, Massachusetts

Elenita Chickering Collection
1869 [1977–1994] 2003

Accession #2003.050

Date: September 2, 2004
Processing date: Melissa Mannon, Archives Consultant

Collection size: 12 cubic feet

Access: This collection is open to researchers without restriction. To view the collection, contact the Gardner Museum at 28 Pearl Street, Gardner, Massachusetts 01440. Tel. 978-632-3277.

Copyright: Permission to publish from the collection must be obtained from Trustees of the Gardner Museum. Permission to publish from secondary sources (including published materials, copies of archival material, and duplicate photographs from other collections) must be obtained from the owner(s) of the original documents. Consult officials at the Gardner Museum for more information.

Scope and Content Note

This collection includes the writings, notes, photographs, and correspondence of Elenita Chickering that relate to her study of the life and work of silversmith Arthur J. Stone. The bulk of the material was gathered or created as Chickering prepared for the writing of her monumental study of Stone. Her book, entitled *Arthur J. Stone, 1847–1938, Designer and Silversmith*, is the most comprehensive study of the master craftsman and has been recognized as an outstanding look into the life of an artist. The materials in Chickering's archival collection not only provide additional information about the artist, but also shed light on the efforts of an author to undertake such a work and to get it published.

For those interested in Chickering's work, the most interesting and enlightening archival documents in this collection are her correspondence, edited writings, and research notes. They tell us much about the passion of the woman for her comprehensive study of the famous silversmith. These documents make up a large portion of the material found here. The correspondence, which includes letters to and from famous silversmiths, silver experts, and private collectors, also tells us much about Stone. Many of the correspondents were personally acquainted with the artist or have special knowledge of his work. The correspondence served as a way to record what they knew in order to assist Chickering with her work and provide personal recollections of Stone's shop that are not found elsewhere.

The collection also includes much secondary source material, which can be extremely useful to those researching the life of Arthur J. Stone. Primarily composed of photocopies made by Elenita Chickering for her research, the nonarchival documents in this collection gather information from diverse sources, including various museum, library, and private collections. A sample of these materials includes copies of Stone exhibition checklists, articles about Stone and silversmithing, museum inventories of Stone silver, photographs of items owned by various repositories, and copies of archival documents owned by other repositories.

Photographs in this collection relate to Chickering's research and are mostly duplicates of those found in other repositories or in private collections, while some are snapshots that were taken by Chickering for her studies. Period ephemera make up a small portion of this collection. It includes primarily sales catalogues of silver, exhibit brochures, museum flyers, and conference materials.

Notable items in the collection include a copy of Stone's will located in the "Front Matter" section of the first series. A few copies of original correspondence written by Arthur Stone and his wife Elizabeth are interspersed in the "Plans for Publication" series. Original Elizabeth Stone correspondence was given to Chickering by William B. Rhoads and can be found in the correspondence series in the "Rhoads" folder. Another interesting document is Arthur J. Stone's indenture to Edwin Eagle for silversmithing in the series entitled "Research—The Early Years." An original and signed drawing by Arthur J. Stone of an ecclesiastical chalice is included in the "Ecclesiastical Silver 1905–1911" folder. Also notable in this series is Chickering's correspondence with her cousin Alma Bent, which includes information about the author's early book plans.

Biographical Note

Elenita Cowee Chickering is the grandniece of Elizabeth Bent Stone, wife of the silversmith Arthur J. Stone. Chickering spent time with Stone during her childhood, staying summers at the Stone home in Gardner, Massachusetts. She began her formal study of the artist in the 1970s, when she desired to learn more about this interesting family member. In 1981, Chickering was the guest curator of the Arthur Stone silver exhibition at the Boston Athenaeum entitled *Arthur J. Stone: Handwrought Silver, 1901–1937*. She subsequently went on to produce the full monograph on Stone entitled *Arthur J. Stone 1847–1938, Designer and Silversmith*. She is the recognized authority on artist Arthur J. Stone.

According to Ms. Chickering's monograph on the artist, Arthur J. Stone (1847–1938) was "one of the last independent American silversmiths to make silver by hand." He was born in Sheffield, England, where he began an apprenticeship to master silversmith Edwin Eagle at the age of fourteen. After his apprenticeship, Stone worked in England for some years at James Dixon and Sons. In 1884, he immigrated to the United States and worked for William B. Durgin Company of Concord, New Hampshire. He later worked for Frank W. Smith Silver Company in Gardner, and Howard and Company in New York. Stone finally established a shop of his own in Gardner, Massachusetts, in 1901, where he became a respected member of the Boston Society of Arts and Crafts.

Series Descriptions

Series 1—Plans for Publication

The first series relates to plans for publication and was originally located in ten loose-leaf notebooks. Chickering referred to these records as "Monograph Material." It includes the following subseries: "Front Matter, Text and Notes"; "Monograph"; "Domestic Hollowware 1901–07, 1908–13, 1919–20, 1925–37"; "Illustration Captions"; "End Matter." Within this series can be found photographs of artwork, Stone family photographs, photograph captions, correspondence (including primarily permissions to reproduce photographs), and notes regarding plans for the book.

Series 2—Research

Extensive research material reflecting Chickering's work was located in an additional twenty-nine notebooks that were donated to the Gardner Museum after the original series. This material was gathered during the course of many years of research about Stone and was not necessarily assembled specifically for the book. The subseries include: "Book Drafts"; "Catalogues of Stone's Work"; "Articles"; "Pyx"; "Ecclesiastical Silver"; "Presentation Pieces"; "Exhibitions"; and "Research." The "Pyx" series includes information about a small wafer box used by priests for sacramental rites in sickness. Stone and several other Boston Society of Arts and Crafts members created this particular pyx for the Church of the Advent in Boston. The "Ecclesiastical Silver" series includes text copy, notes, and photos about silver made for religious institutions by Stone. There is also appraisal information for some of the pieces.

Series 3—Correspondence

This large series consisting primarily of correspondence was originally organized into six file boxes. It was donated after the first two series. As Ms. Chickering researched Stone's life, she corresponded with people who had expertise about certain aspects of his work or who owned work created during a certain period. The "Correspondence" series reflects her back-and-forth exchanges with many silver experts, collectors, and artists who worked with Stone and discusses particular pieces created by the famous artist. The correspondence also includes copies of letters sent out by Chickering to these people. Interspersed throughout this series are some ephemera, articles, photographs, draft text for the book, and research material related to silver.

Arrangement

The collection reflects the original arrangement of Elenita Chickering. Marnie Nicholson originally described portions of this collection. Her original "fond description" is attached. The entire collection has been fully processed by archival consultant Melissa Mannon to meet archival standards. Archival folders for the first two series, which were originally housed in notebooks, have been labeled with the original notebook numbers to reflect their original arrangement.

Originally arranged in loose-leaf notebooks, book-related materials have been removed from the original housing and placed in archival boxes and folders. The collection was donated in three sets. According to a letter dated January 31, 2004, to Dorothy Tracy by Elenita Chickering, the first set of notebooks included ten binders of materials related to the publication of her book prior to editing by the Boston Athenaeum. The notebooks were arranged by book section. The largest book section, entitled "Domestic Hollowware," was arranged in notebooks by date.

The second set of twenty-nine notebooks included Ms. Chickering's research. Information in each subseries relates to specific periods of Stone's life and work and reflects Chickering's research about these specific periods. The dates on folders do not reflect the time during which original materials in the series (primarily correspondence, notes, and writings) of Chickering were created, but rather reflect when Chickering performed her research.

The third series, which is made up primarily of correspondence, is generally organized by the last name of the correspondent. However, if a person was particularly close to Chickering, that person's correspondence is filed under the correspondent's first name (example: Alma Bent in the "A" section). Some of the folders are labeled with the name of the institution at which the correspondent worked, rather than the name of the person or the name of the subject of the material if it is not correspondence. Additional correspondence is interspersed with research materials. The name index in this finding aid should serve as a guide to help the user locate individuals whose material can be found in the numerous collection locations. Within the "Correspondence" series are some folders of other types of materials. Though this material is not correspondence, its alphabetical arrangement makes it most appropriate for the material to remain here rather than being moved to the seemingly more appropriate "Research" series, which has a chronological arrangement.

In addition, much material in this collection can be found duplicated from series to series, demonstrating the organizational methods Chickering used to perform her study of Arthur J. Stone. Duplicates found from series to series have not been discarded and reflect the multiple access points Chickering used to find her research information.

Post-it notes attached to pages have been photocopied. The original Post-it notes have been discarded and the copies retained for preservation purposes. Chickering also kept many notes on index cards that have been photocopied for preservation purposes.

Additional Finding Aids

Chickering created item-level inventories for the chronological notebooks. They are attached to this finding aid as an addendum. Also attached as an addendum is a correspondence index created by Chickering for the "Correspondence" series. The list does not fully reflect the folders the archivist found in the collection while processing it. Other indices created by Chickering are interfiled in the collection in front of the subseries they describe. They were originally filed this way by the author.

An index for the correspondence found in the collection was created by the consulting archivist. It includes names of people who wrote to Elenita Chickering. It does not necessarily include all the people to whom Chickering wrote, though many copies of her outgoing correspondence are included in the series.

Box and Folder List

SERIES ONE—PLANS FOR PUBLICATION

Box 1—Monograph Notebooks

Monograph Notebook 1—Front Matter
Monograph Notebook 1—Part I Monograph
Monograph Notebook 2—Monograph Continued
Monograph Notebook 3—Domestic Hollowware—1901–07   (2 folders)
Monograph Notebook 4—   1908–13
Monograph Notebook 5—   1919–20
Monograph Notebook 6—   1925–37

Box 2—Monograph Notebooks (cont.)

Monograph Notebook 7—Illustration Captions (family photos and notes)
Monograph Notebook 8—2nd Illustration Captions Notebook (shop photos)
Monograph Notebook 9—More Illustration Captions
Monograph Notebook 10—End Matter and Miscellaneous

Box 3—Second Draft of Book, Catalogues of Stone's Work, Articles

Book—2nd draft (partially edited), 1995
Catalogue of Stone's Work, Worcester Art Museum
Catalogue of Stones Work (and notes)—Museum of Fine Arts, Boston (2 folders)
Articles about Stone (not foldered)

Box 4—Pyx

Photographs and Data
Photographs and Data—Clive Russ
Correspondence, 1977–83
Boston Athenaeum Exhibit of Advent's Vestments and Plate, 1983
Research—*Golden Age of Hispanic Silver*
Tiller article with research   (2 folders)

Mental and Writing Exercises for Describing Information

1. Look at a set of organized records in your home. Identify an alternate arrangement for it. For example, if it is filed by subject, could it alternatively have been filed chronologically?

2. Think about why a particular arrangement was chosen and applied to your records. What advantages and disadvantages would an alternate arrangement have? How can you overcome any disadvantages by creating a finding aid?

3. Have you already created useful alternate access tools for your collections? Have you created family trees or digital databases for records or photographs?

4. Describe how the records in your household came under your care. Are they all products of your life, or did they come from someone else? Where have they been stored? When were they given to you?

5. Create a description of your collection. In paragraph form or as a bulleted list, explain the contents of the collection. Add context by explaining how materials relate to each other and to larger cultural events.

6. Use your personal collection as a launching point for writing a short personal biography in paragraph form, as a bulleted list, or as a timeline.

7. Based on your knowledge of the life of the individual(s) represented in your records, is the collection missing any important information? Could materials reflecting this information be housed somewhere else? List other places where one might find information about the person(s) represented in your collection (whether it's you or a family member or members).

Chapter Five: Preserving Personal Papers

Introduction to Preservation

"Preservation" in the archives field is the discipline that helps ensure the longevity of historical resources. All organic items (including papers) inevitably degrade over time. Our job is to delay their deterioration as much as we can—to make the decay of materials slow to an imperceptible rate. This chapter describes the causes of decay and provides information about methods to retard its impact.

The rate of deterioration depends on a combination of factors, including environment, storage materials, and the chemical composition of an item itself. Diverse personal archives have varied needs. This chapter highlights some of the most common materials found in one's home and discusses various factors that may cause them peril. I encourage you to aim for good conditions. It is difficult to achieve perfection in the average residence. The more factors you can control to create a more hospitable home for your family collection, the higher the likelihood that your materials will survive to be passed from generation to generation.

This chapter is an outgrowth of a presentation that I have run for

Common Preservation Problems

- Food particles attract bugs, which then move on to the starch-filled cloth, paper, and tasty glues in old books and documents.
- Acids from newsprint cause discoloration and embrittlement of adjacent pages in scrapbooks and other treasured home items.
- Vinyl pages and adhesive from "magnetic" albums adhere to photos and turn them yellow.
- Paper that was commonly used in old scrapbooks yellows and becomes so brittle that it breaks along the edges, damaging the cherished items that it is supposed to protect.
- A damp basement or attic provides an ideal climate for encouraging insects and mold growth, while causing books to warp and papers to expand and cockle.
- Paper clips rust, wrinkling paper and leaving their brown imprint.
- Pressure-sensitive tapes, rubber cement, and glue used to repair torn pages or to adhere items at home, cause items to discolor.

the past ten years called "Preserving Memories." I provide information about what items one commonly finds in one's home and how to best protect these materials. People are invited to bring in their own personal papers and photographs to discuss their condition. I help them determine what actions can be taken to prolong the life of these items. In this chapter, I try to address the questions that are most commonly asked. I discuss the basics a nonprofessional needs to consider to avoid damaging personal papers, photographs, and memorabilia without providing all-encompassing preservation information. For those who wish to learn more, the bibliography includes professional publications that provide wide-ranging and specific information about most of the problems one may come up against in an archives repository.

We Do What We Can

In my first full-time professional archives position, my archives storage area was not perfect. The Archives had been renovated only recently and was moved up from the basement level to the main building level. I was a lucky archivist in a beautiful sunny facility, while most of my colleagues in other institutions complained about basement storage with no windows. I was soon even given my own office with my own bathroom to boot. After a short time, I went to my director and told him that some things needed to change. I explained that the boxes would offer some protection to the materials from the bright Palladian windows in my storage area, but my bathroom pipes ran over the area, too. I wanted to sacrifice my bathroom to protect the resources. I asked my patient boss to consider shutting off the pipes in my space so we could avoid a potential disaster. In one of my first professional lessons, my boss told me that the renovation work on the building was through and he was not going to shut down my bathroom. I have since learned that the ideal is not always feasible in diverse situations. We do the best we can.

Keeping Ephemera

In Chapter Two, I discussed the value of ephemera for contributing to the context of one's life story. The cigarette trading-card book I described from my Bermuda vacation is not unique, but it reminds me of a special time and place. It also relates to the topic of English history, which I find enthralling and the love of which is one of my quirky characteristics. For these reasons, this item is special to me. Most of the items in my "personal archives" were created by me, about me, or by a loved one. The ephemera I have kept—including such things as tickets from shows and postcards from places I have visited—fit none of these categories. They do help fill out my story by showing what is meaningful to me and the activities in which I take part.

Ephemera are not meant to last. They usually serve a one-time purpose to inform or to get people interested in something. Ephemera are usually made of cheap materials with no concern for permanence. This makes it particularly difficult for us to try to prolong their lifespan. The cigarette cards are part of my personal memorabilia, along with other vacation mementos and items such as the certificates I won as a child and the brochures I pick up on museum visits. These items have personal significance to me, but they have less meaning to others if reviewed out of context.

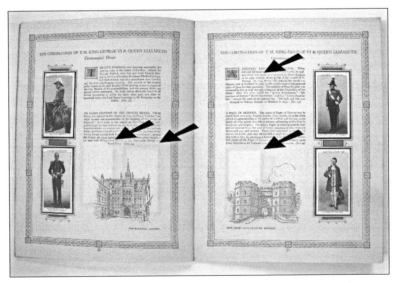

Figure 22. The arrows on this page point to places where ink from the cards has migrated from one page to the other.

My little souvenir is in relatively good condition, especially considering that I found it housed in a small shop on an extremely humid island—a condition highly detrimental to the longevity of archival material. There are two prime preservation issues with the booklet. The places to glue the cards are bordered by a beautiful burgundy frame, which you unfortunately cannot see in these black-and-white pictures. They appear on the previous page as a thick black line around each person's image. The red ink has migrated from their page onto the facing pages; I have drawn arrows to point to the places where this has occurred. The second issue is that the staples holding the book together have rusted and are causing small areas of discoloration on the paper.

The damp island conditions may have been the prime factor in causing these problems. I have moved the book to a cool and less humid New England home, where we keep air conditioning in the summer and heat in the winter, creating a relatively stable climate that prolongs the life of materials. Cool temperatures slow

Finding the Best Space in Your Home to Store Materials

- Keep materials cool, dry, and dark.
- Keep the temperature below 72 degrees.
- Keep humidity between 30 percent and 50 percent.
- Maintain stable temperature and humidity, even if you are unable to keep ideal specific settings.
- Keep personal papers out of attics, basements, and garages, where conditions can fluctuate dramatically.
- Keep air conditioning on in the summer and take advantage of winter weather to keep things cool.
- If the building in which you keep your materials cannot be cooled, try to find a room with as stable an environment as possible. Interior rooms are your best bet, as rooms along outer walls of an edifice are more vulnerable to the fluctuations that occur outside.
- Use a dehumidifier or a humidifier if necessary.
- An unstable environment, especially high temperatures and humidity levels, accelerates damage to materials.
- Keep items in a box to create a more stable "micro-climate."

Basic Items Used for Safe Storage of Archival Materials

Buffered/lignin-free document storage boxes—one-half-cubic-foot or three-cubic-foot for standard letter-sized documents. (Consider special boxes for legal-sized manuscripts; flat boxes for oversized and brittle materials; and appropriately sized photo storage boxes.)

Buffered/lignin-free file folders—legal or letter-sized with varying tabs, depending on your preference.

Buffered/lignin-free "interleaving" papers—to use between brittle or acidic pages or to fold into envelopes for smaller materials. Standard sheets or tissue.

Preservation-quality envelopes in a variety of sizes—a fancier and often more supportive way to store brittle or small items.

Polyester (Melinex) enclosures (folders, pockets, or envelopes)—for brittle documents or photographs.

Document box supports—ensure materials stand upright even when box is not full. One can use a curved folder to support materials in lieu of a specialized support.

Number 2 pencils and a good eraser, such as Staedtler Mars or Sanford Magic Rub.

deterioration and save energy so zoned heating and set-backs that allow you to lower temperatures to save money will also help preserve your archives collections.

I found the booklet in a plastic sleeve, which is a common enclosure for many items we peruse at antique shops. This primary storage, which directly touches treasured items, is a major contributing factor in materials' deterioration. I have re-housed my booklet in a new folder as its first level of protection, and I have placed the folder in a box. Both the box and folder are buffered and lignin-free to provide a stable environment that will not harm the items.[40]

I suspect that the climate and the supplies used to house the items were not the only causes of this particular item's

---

[40] Buffered materials have an alkaline reserve, usually calcium carbonate, that neutralizes the effect of acids in archival material, slowing deterioration.

deterioration. It seems likely to me that the red ink on the cards is acidic and will continue to make marks where they do not belong if I am not careful. Because of this, I have placed thin sheets of paper between the pages so if the ink bleeds, it will discolor the papers and not the book pages themselves. I check the sheets periodically to see if any red has transferred onto them. So far, after ten years, it has not. But if it did, I would regularly change the interleaving sheets to remove the contamination. These "interleaving" pages work well in a small booklet like this but probably would not work as well for a tightly bound book where their presence may cause the item to be overstuffed, placing unwanted stress on the binding.

I have left my rusty staples in place for now. The rust is not eating through the pages, the staples hold the book together nicely, and the discoloration has not gotten any worse over ten years. I do have the option to carefully remove the staples with one of my favorite tools: A microspatula is handy for this purpose when necessary. Certain things in preservation are a judgment call. I do not want to cause more damage by removing staples. Their presence does not seem to be causing any more harm now that other factors have been changed.

The Unique Needs of Newsprint

Newsprint is so acidic that the best preservation step is to make copies onto acid-free paper, either by scanning or photocopying, if you want to keep this information. Retain copies and discard originals if they are loose. Large piles of newspapers that are stored together in the dark are often in better condition than small clippings because they are shielded from air and light. As soon as modern newsprint is exposed to light and air, it turns yellow and becomes brittle. The rapidity of the deterioration is due to the fact that newsprint is produced from ground wood that contains lignin and has not been purified. Newspapers printed before the advent of wood pulp are in better condition and safer to keep with your standard documents.

Diverse Papers

In Chapter Two, I briefly introduced letters that my mother sent me while I was in college. I retain a folder of these materials that illustrate an important time in my life and the changing of an important relationship in my life. In the 1960s, "social history" gained respect and importance as a field of study because researchers began studying the "average" person and not just the famous to better understand history and society. My letters are among many types of materials in people's homes that tell us more about life in the 1980s, mother-daughter relationships, college women, and similar subjects. Like my diaries, photographs and other materials that I create in my day-to-day activities, these papers describe me, my family, my communities, and the culture that surrounds my life.

Correspondence is commonly found among most home collections, and our impulse to save it is usually quite strong. Many of us have letters from important people in our lives, yet we rarely consider the best way to store it. Airmail, postcards, expensive letterhead, notepaper, and greeting cards are made of diverse materials that sometimes have diverse needs that deserve consideration. We do things such as gently tie our letters with pretty ribbon or put them in a cigar box. This is storage that adds to a sense of historical mystique, but it does nothing to prolong the items' longevity.

The first step in keeping papers is to make sure that you have a first line of protection. Make the items' primary storage an enclosure such as a file folder. The file folder keeps things neat and provides support for your documents. Unfold pages to avoid weakening folds. I often find letters in archives that have been torn along these spots. If tearing has occurred, do not use pressure-sensitive tape (also known as adhesive tape, sticky tape, and by the "Scotch" brand); this tape may cause further damage. Torn items may be placed in polyester pockets or folders, where static electricity holds them in place. See the section on conservation treatment for details about repair. If possible, use folders or envelopes that are appropriately sized for your materials in letter-sized or legal-sized formats. I keep a few legal-sized letters from my mother with one side folded so they fit in a letter-sized box. I do not have the space to keep these letters separated following my best-case guidelines. This is a case where I do what I can without achieving perfection. I know that because they are folded, these letters may tear along the fold line more easily than other materials in the collection, but that is a chance I feel I can take.

As I place materials in folders, I pay attention to their physical makeup. I separate items that are slightly yellowing on the edges, papers made with colored dyes, and papers with bleeding inks from others by using interleaving sheets. Buffered/lignin-free white pages help prevent the deleterious components from migrating across sheets. I remove items with obvious signs of acidity, such as yellowing or brittleness. I discard or store these papers separately. I put a note with the other materials that I have done that or make a copy to put in its place.

For example, my mother is fond of comic strips. She sent me a few when I was in college to highlight how she was feeling or just to give me a chuckle. The comics are meaningful to me for this reason, but also because they remind me that she also taped comics to the wall next to the refrigerator in my childhood home. I remember them yellowing and curling on the edges, straining against the adhesive tape she used to affix them to the wall. To prevent the deterioration of the newsprint-based items in my "Mom's Letters" series of papers, I have made photocopies, tossing the original in favor of preserving the memory rather than trying to protect the original that has no inherent value to me.

Figure 23. One of Mom's letters, unfolded and looking as it did the day she wrote it twenty years ago.

"Mom's Letters" take up no more than one small folder among my personal papers. So, I have retained greeting cards (my mom is also fond of those) and other small items among larger sheets of paper. To keep these items from being tossed around and to maintain organization, I place small items in buffered/lignin-free envelopes or create my own special enclosures by folding interleaving paper in half and placing small items within it. This method is handy for keeping similar items together instead of using possibly harmful paper clips or staples.

Boxes provide the next level of protection for collections after folders and other enclosures. As a secondary storage defense, boxes shield items from dust and light. They also provide some protection against outside pollutants, pests, water, and changes in temperature and humidity. Archives boxes come in any size you can imagine to appropriately fit materials. Make sure materials fit securely and do not slide in enclosures. Use flat boxes for oversized items. Use either one-half-cubic-foot document boxes or three-cubic-foot record storage cartons for legal- or letter-sized manuscripts. Store archives in these boxes upright in their folders. Do not overstuff containers. Boxes are also made for artifacts of all sizes. Many have compartments serving specialized purposes for the storage of fabrics, jewelry, natural specimens, and the like. Because of their diverse needs, separate your personal memorabilia from your archives and keep them in suitable boxes.

Figure 24. A page from the baby book that suckered me into preserving my memories in a less than ideal way.

Making Do with the Materials You Have

Most of us have items such as: locks of hair, documentation of first words, baby shoes, and birth/weight statistics. Ideally, when seeking to preserve your treasured memories, start with safe materials. Purchase albums and storage boxes from reputable archival supply companies.[41] Record your information properly right from the start.

When my daughter was born, I received a cute baby book from a friend. I would have thanked the person kindly and then purchased a buffered/lignin-free journal if I had thought deeply about it. Few of us consider such things when we are caught in a family moment. I was pulled in by cuteness and used the pretty little baby book to record all the early memories of my daughter's life. The book sat on a wooden shelf for eight years. The once pearl-white pages now seem to be turning a barely perceptible delicate cream.

The best that I can do is "make do" and change a few things I've been doing to increase the item's longevity. I now keep the book flat in a proper box to prevent the excess strain on the pages. I keep the item away from light and in a stable climate. I plan to digitize the pages so I have an extra copy.

Tucked inside the book is a list of my daughter's first 100 words or so. They are written on a page pulled from a legal pad; each word is written in a different color ink. I remember waiting and waiting for the word "Ma" to come out of her mouth as I wrote new words each day. This piece of paper is one of the most special things I have ever recorded, despite my ill-conceived method of documentation. Although I can reformat the list by typing, photocopying, or scanning it, this original document has significance to me. I will make a second

---

[41] See the "Archives Supplies" section on page 140 for more information on this topic.

Scrapbooking

Scrapbooking is a popular way to display valued family mementoes, but it is not a preservation method. Scrapbooking breaks one of the basic tenets of caring for your treasured family papers: Avoid doing anything that is irreversible to them.

However, I am a proponent of focusing on your items in this way to encourage appreciation of your personal story, if you are keen on the idea. Instead of cutting up and gluing irreplaceable items into scrapbooks, consider making copies of photographs, original certificates, and other unique items. Since your ephemera do not hold exceptional value, you may choose to use these items in your albums. Keep your archival originals in archival boxes so they are secure for posterity.

The scrapbooks you create become valuable family documentation unto themselves. Their form, your hard work, and your point of view deserve special care, too. Many scrapbook vendors are serious about "archival-quality" supplies. *Creative Memories™*, in particular, was one of the first companies to focus on preservation-safe methods and worked with specialists in the archives world to help ensure that their supplies would not harm yours. Materials should stay stable so they do not discolor or come apart over time. Hold scrapbook suppliers to the same standards you hold vendors of other archives supplies.

"preservation copy," but I will leave the original tucked inside my book with baby hair and other items and thoughts that remind me of my baby's first years. There is something to be said for personal papers as artifacts that touch us by their physical form as well as their contents. One must be aware of the risks and weigh their potential against the value of the story in a personal collection. Keeping these items in a stable environment, in a special box, off of a wooden shelf that can give off harmful vapors, and away from light will likely be just enough to keep this particular item safe.

Conserving Damaged Materials

Our discussion thus far has focused on preservation steps to prolong the usable life of your collections and prevent further damage. Sometimes, however, we are too late and items are already torn, stained, or badly curled. Books can have powdery leather, detached covers, and loose pages. Although the tendency is to reach for the Scotch tape, the preferred step is to consult a conservation professional.

Conservation refers to the care and treatment of the physical object. Its practitioners are known as conservators, and they undergo a rigorous master's program or apprenticeship in the science and craft of their specialties, which may include paper, books, and photographs. Conservators are able to analyze problems and propose solutions that will stabilize structure and repair damage

If your item is valuable, either financially or personally, it is preferable to hire a conservator to perform the treatment than to attempt an amateur repair on your own. While conservation is not inexpensive, undoing bad repairs performed with tape, Elmer's Glue™, or rubber cement will be far more costly. Many conservators give verbal estimates, but be sure to ask in advance about charges. If you cannot afford immediate specialty treatment, simple boxing is better than a poor repair.

Conservators and Disaster Specialists

Archivists are trained in preservation, which involves avoiding elements that lead to the deterioration of materials. Conservation is a specialized field that involves alleviating or fixing damage that has occurred. A conservator evaluates the condition of your damaged items and treats them. Many are also specialists in disaster recovery and prevention, or preparedness, working side-by-side with archivists in this area. A bookbinder with conservation training and experience can be a good option for your bound materials.

The American Institute for Conservation, Washington, D.C.: www.conservation-us.org (See their online tool for locating an independent conservator in your area.)

Regional Alliance for Preservation, a network of nonprofit conservators: www.rap-arcc.org

Preservation Standards

Standards-testing bodies include the ASTM International (formerly known as the American Society for Testing and Materials), the ISO (International Organization for Standardization), and ANSI (American National Standards Institute). See www.iso.org, www.astm.org, and www.ansi.org. Look for these when choosing supplies:

ASTM D3290—"Permanent" paper. Carries the symbol ∞. Relatively chemically stable and undergoes a very slow rate of deterioration.

ISO 9706—"Permanent" paper.

ISO 11108—"Archival" paper. An especially durable version of permanent paper used for documentation of high importance.

ISO 18916—"Passes PAT." The PAT (Photographic Activity Test) deems materials are stable and safe for the storage of photographs. For more on the Photographic Activity Test, see www.imagepermanenceinstitute.org/testing/pat.

Archives Supplies

Unfortunately, there are no recognizable terms that will tell you a particular supply is safe for your items. Many manufacturers use words such as "Archival" or "Preservation Safe" to market their products. There are suppliers who have made it their profession to develop products for the archives, library, and museum communities and you should seek these rather than relying on nebulous terms.

The following companies are reputable archival suppliers that cater to the needs of professionals and individuals:

- *Conservation Resources*™ www.conservationresources.com
- *Gaylord Brothers*™ www.gaylord.com
- *Hollinger Metal Edge*™ www.hollingermetaledge.com
- *Talas*™ www.talasonline.com
- *University Products*™ www.universityproducts.com

Certain high-end frame shops and art stores carry preservation supplies in small quantities. Look for trade names such as *Lineco*™ and terms such as "buffered and lignin-free" or "PAT" for photographic storage. These references show a greater understanding of archival issues by manufacturers.

Photographs

One of the most common items that require special preservation attention in our homes is a photograph. The diversity of the photographic process makes the requirements for maintaining these items just as varied. From early images created with newly discovered chemical processes, to unstable color images, to high-volume and quickly changing digital technology, the preservation of photographs is a specialized field unto itself.

My childhood images are photographs from the 1970s. A prime time for Polaroids and one-hour film processing, this decade also marked the apex of the use of the "magnetic" photo album. The chemicals used to develop images instantly combined with the poor glues and plastics in my album, causing my items to fade and discolor in a relatively short twenty-year time frame. I have removed them and placed them in a better album to keep them secure.

Figure 25. My photo album from the 1970s quickly discolored and faded. I removed images and re-housed them to slow the deterioration.

Seek to have treasured photographic prints in poor condition copied and reprinted with high-quality photographic papers and inks.[42] Be wary of the materials we use to print at home today. Look for high-quality photo printers rather than small machines that can print fast. These fast machines usually attract buyers with their ease, but they are poor preservation choices. Choose professional photo studios over big-box stores, mall photo shops, and low-quality mail order for higher-quality prints.

Be sure to use preservation supplies that were made with a particular regard to their photo storage safety. Use materials that have passed the Photographic Activity Test (PAT). These items have been tested to determine their suitability for storing images and to ensure that they do not contain chemical

---

[42] Wilhelm Imaging Research is the respected authority on print permanence. See its website with in-depth articles about archival inks at www.wilhelm-research.com.

additives or coatings that can harm photographs. Also avoid plastic materials with PVCs. Plastics that are safe to use with photographs are polyester, polyethylene, and polypropylene. Polyester is clear and rigid (and more expensive), making it ideal for items that are fragile and handled frequently. Polyethylene and polypropylene are softer and less clear, but much less expensive. Again, purchase your plastics from a reputable supplier who has done the research and selected products that are pure.

Figure 26. Photo album from the mid-twentieth century using common black paper and photo corners.

This is another example of a common twentieth-century issue with photographs. I found the above album at an antique shop. The relatively stable black-and-white prints are countered by the highly acidic black pages on which they are mounted. The images are beginning to discolor around the edges. Luckily, the photos themselves have not been glued to the pages and can be removed easily from the album. It is a great idea to use photo corners such as these for this reason. The images here can be placed in a new, safe album or stored in a photo box.

Sometimes people feel attached to the format in which their images are kept and not just to the images themselves. They wish to retain an album for sentimental reasons. Evaluate how much the album really means to you. If it is causing the images distress, consider removing the photographs and storing the album separately. You might also consider photographing or scanning each page before dismantling it to "preserve" how the album looks intact. For fancy albums that you wish to keep as they are, consult a conservator for treatment options. These are likely to be expensive, but this alternative may be justifiable for highly prized albums.

Many families have images that were made one hundred years ago or more. Daguerreotypes, ambrotypes, and tintypes have specialized storage needs. Retain items in their original cases and stand upright in appropriate boxes. People often ask what to do with loose tintypes in my workshops. Store them safely upright and individually in pH-neutral envelopes or inert plastic enclosures. If possible, replace storage cases. Contact a conservator for more intense restoration of these images or to repair ambrotypes and daguerreotypes, which are more fragile.

Scanning Images

Image courtesy of Kerrie Van Dalsum.

You can scan old photographs with some deterioration and digitally enhance them. You can even make them look new. I have removed brown spots and discoloration from this photograph to make a clean black-and-white appearance. You can retain original sepia tones for a nostalgic effect, but you may also choose a cleaner appearance. After scanning, protect originals using preservation supplies. Print and display scanned versions without fear of deterioration.

"Preserving" a Photo's Informational Value

Figure 27. Unlabeled and unknown, this photograph provides photographer information that gives us a clue into the identity of these girls.

Although not technically a "preservation" issue, next to properly creating images and using safe storage supplies, there is nothing more important to a photo's long-term security than identification. You may preserve family treasures using recognized safe methods, but they may be useless to future generations without some information tying the photo or item to your life. Be sure to record the names of the people pictured, the event, and the date the photo was taken. Keep notes about your precious materials near the preserved items. Use a preservation-safe pen or pencil on the back of the image along the bottom edge. Be careful not to bear down and leave an impression on the front. Record information on the storage supplies if you are sure the supplies will not get separated from the images themselves.

The methods of identifying images are somewhat controversial. While we never want to do anything irreversible to our archives, labeling images in erasable pencil often does not work on a photo's slick surface. Early photographs were printed on paper that takes pencil easily. Modern photograph papers are resin-coated, creating a glossy surface that does not take pencil well. Archivists have differing opinions on how to handle labeling when a pencil is not an option. Avoid using a ballpoint pen. Consider preservation-safe pens purchased from a reputable archives supplier. These are made from neutral inks that are supposed to keep your materials from harm, but their use is obviously not reversible. Other archivists use labels that supposedly have safe glues to stick on the back of your images, but these labels sometimes fall off and can get separated from items as the glue changes over time. Another option is to slip photos in appropriate plastic envelops and place labels on the envelopes, but there is a stronger possibility of losing that information—sometime down the road, the item may get separated from its housing. All in all, there is no one perfect way to label images. Find a method that works for you and keeps your items as safe as possible, but be sure to label!

The technology for creating photographs is rapidly changing. We are in danger of losing many of our most precious images. Lost among hard drives with thousands of unidentified images or stuffed in shoeboxes full of similarly unlabeled prints, photographs possess limited value. Keep track of your original images, both printed and not printed. Store original images safely, and mark them appropriately. Make copies for displaying, sharing, and as preservation backups to ensure their longevity. A little extra attention will ensure that materials are there when you want to see them in their original splendor with all the identifiers one would need to recognize their value.

Labeling and Preserving

In the picture above, my grandmother looks at an unidentified little girl. It is the only picture my family owns of this child. We believe this girl may be the older sister of my mother. The sibling died during World War II before my mother was born. The image remains a giant mystery and a source of heartache. It would be wonderful if I knew for sure that this is an image of my aunt, but the photo is unlabeled. I used a graphics editing program to retouch the photo. I keep the original paper image stored away. I keep the digital original and the backup altered copy for preservation. I hope that we decipher the image's real story one day.

Preserving Audio-Visual Material

I have a set of cassette tapes stored in an archives box that I am afraid to touch. The summer after my freshman year, I was separated from my boyfriend, who is now my husband. It was the last summer that we would ever spend apart. I missed him. I missed his voice. He sent me recordings so I could hear him whenever I wanted. It would be lovely to hear the voice of the man I now hear every day and to be reminded of young love, but I am afraid that I would hear a crackly mess. Or I am afraid that I might snap the tape if I try to play it. I am not even sure that I have a decent machine in the house to play it without chewing it up.

VHS tapes, 8mm, Betacam, and other analog magnetic media are highly unstable and prone to degradation. Like other materials, the longevity of formats varies depending in part on storage conditions, handling, and the processes under which the materials are created. The degradation of this format is noteworthy for a "sticky tape" phenomenon that involves components of the item becoming soft and/or brittle, even among higher-quality tapes.[43] Degrading tapes also sometimes give off a faint vinegar smell, which indicates that the backing of the tapes is in poor condition.

Figure 28. Small collections of magnetic media are prevalent among family collections, but many cannot access their information due to the instability of the media.

To try to increase the longevity of items that remain in good condition within your family collection, store recordings at a temperature of between 60 and 68 degrees Fahrenheit and keep it stable. Maintain a relative humidity of 25 percent to 45 percent. As

---

[43] For more information on caring for audio-visual materials, see John Van Bogart's "Magnetic Tape Storage and Handling: A Guide for Libraries and Archives," National Media Laboratory, June 1995, www.clir.org/pubs/reports/pub54/1introduction.html (July 27, 2011).

with all archives, fluctuations in temperature and humidity are the biggest climate factors for degradation. Maintain proper ventilation and air circulation at all times. Keep sound recordings in dark storage when not being consulted. Avoid pollutants and handling as much as possible. Keep materials upright rather than storing them flat. Do not store them on electronic equipment, which may harm the magnetic field.

When following these procedures, materials should be reviewed regularly for signs of degradation. Visually evaluate the tape itself for tackiness, brittleness, and shrinkage. If you want to try to play items on a recorder to see if they are still in good condition, make sure the device that you are using to play them is clean. Do not use rewind or fast-forward functions that increase the possibility of the tape snapping. Rewind an item by hand. If you have not played a tape in some time, consider bringing the recording to a professional rather than playing it yourself to avoid a mishap. Also consult a conservator if tape emits an odor.

The problem of degrading media is accompanied by the need for a device to play analog tapes, which is often difficult, as technology has changed dramatically over the past decade. Furthermore, the more we play this type of material, the more likely it is to disintegrate. So in just evaluating the condition of an item by playing it, you can degrade its stability. All media should be transferred to new formats as technology changes. Consider digitizing (or have a professional digitize) analog media. Pay attention to changes in innovation, and continually migrate data as old formats become outdated. If you have migrated information once, it does not mean you will not have to migrate it again. Keep copies of audio-visual material on different media and in different formats.[44] If possible, create transcriptions of the materials' content as an additional "backup" of information.

---

[44] See the chapter on electronic information for more on various formats.

"What Papers and Heirlooms Would I Grab from Home during an Emergency?"

Vital records are the documentation that we need to sustain our identity, legal rights, finances, and property. Consider what specific personal records have the greatest informational, evidential, or sentimental impact in your life. If a dramatic event occurs, be prepared to move appropriate items if you are able to do so without endangering yourself. Make sure that everyone in your family knows which personal papers to save by keeping them together in an easy-to-reach place. Consider what is irreplaceable and what you need to easily function from day-to-day.

- Backups of key computer records
- Bank account information, including online user ID and password
- Birth certificates
- Contracts, loans
- Driver's license or photo ID
- Passport
- Insurance records
- Records of household improvements, inventory of goods for insurance
- Immunization records
- Medical history
- Social Security cards
- Marriage and divorce records
- Mortgage records
- Deeds
- Will
- Family photos and history

Disaster Planning

The best thing we can do for disaster planning is preparation. If you consider all of the possible disasters that might affect your region of the country, you can ready yourself for the worst should you find yourself confronted with a potential catastrophe. Families should consider the impact a disaster would have.

Disasters come in many forms. They can include dramatic events such as fires and floods, but they may also include more run-of-the-mill events such as long-term loss of power that affects climate controls and exposes collections to the elements. Disasters that affect your personal papers may include pest infestation or hard-drive failure. Sometimes one disaster can lead to another. For example, a fire can cause water damage when firemen use hoses to put it out or sprinklers are set.

There are some disasters that we can avoid. Regular maintenance of systems and housecleaning can cut down on risks. Make sure fire alarms and extinguishers are in working order. Back up computer files and keep copies off-site. Have your furnace, air conditioner, and other household devices inspected and cleaned annually. We have seen the effects of flooding and other terrible disasters in recent years. A disaster can strike anyone. Considering these potential hazards before an emergency will help avoid panic in a terrible situation.[45]

Figure 29. This is a problem that can be easily avoided, but I see it almost everywhere I go. Records boxed in a basement or attic get damp and moldy. One of your first lines of defense against damage: Keep materials dry in a stable environment (keep temperature and humidity from fluctuating drastically), and prevent additional damage by boxing with appropriate storage supplies.

Figure 30. Pipes running over archives storage areas in your home or in professional repositories are one means of potential disaster.

---

[45] For more information, see the wonderful tip sheet created by the Georgia State Archives, "Essential Records for Families: What You Need to Know before You Evacuate" (sos.georgia.gov/archives/how_may_we_help_you/emergency_advice/evacuation_records.pdf).

Examples of Damage

Light and acid migration from poor storage materials have caused this image to fade.

These items were chewed by a hungry critter.

Tape can discolor materials over time, as seen with the wide strip marks on this atlas.

Factors That Cause Deterioration

Every day, families lose valued memorabilia and personal papers due to neglect, mishandling, and misplacement. Your attentive care can ensure their security. The following is a list of the causes of deterioration. Avoid as many of these harmful factors as you possibly can to prolong the life of your items. Your collections are more likely to be harmed the more these factors are present where you store your materials.

Oxidation—A chemical process caused by an agent such as oxygen in the air, ozone, or pollutants such as nitrogen oxide. Help prevent oxidation by using proper storage methods.

Acids—Acids are chemical agents present in the materials for which you are trying to care and in your storage supplies. Store materials with buffered and lignin-free supplies. Buffered supplies can be beneficial to counteract acidity with many types of materials. These items are impregnated with an alkaline agent to counteract acidity. Check acidity in storage supplies by using a pH-testing pen available from reputable suppliers. Pen marks will change colors depending on the acid content of your supplies. Isolate highly acidic personal items. Be aware that the acidity in inks, like that in paper, can vary and can be a contributing factor in deterioration. Label your materials with pencil or with preservation pens purchased from a reputable supplier.

Environment—Heat and high humidity pose the greatest threats to your collections. Keep conditions cool (below 70 degrees) and dry (between 30-50% RH). Use a hygrometer to monitor; use an air conditioner, humidifier or dehumidifier when necessary.

Fungi—Fungi (which include mold and mildew) are present everywhere and remain dormant as spores until conditions are right for them to bloom.[46] Fungus freely floats in the air, settles on objects, and germinates when excess water is present and environmental conditions are favorable for their proliferation. Keep a stable RH and stable temperature.

Pests—Unwanted creatures can cause damage to collections by chewing materials, making nests in papers and boxes, leaving

Pesky Critters and What They Like

Beetles—wide variety; feed on diverse sources

Cockroaches—feed on everything

Moths—wide variety; feed on diverse sources

Psocids (book lice)—affinity for warm damp places; slow eaters of molds, but can change diets to adapt

Silverfish—particularly fond of starch, such as that found in wood glue; can also damage textiles

Rodents—adapt to feeding on a wide variety of items; prefer moist places

Wood spiders—eat insects found in collections and leave carcasses and eggs; prefer damp environments

(See museumpests.net)

---

[46] According to the American Academy of Microbiology, there are approximately 1.5 million different types of fungi in the world. "The Fungal Kingdom: Diverse and Essential Roles in Earth's Ecosystem," June 2008, academy.asm.org/index.php?option=com_content&view=article&id=222:the-fungal-kingdom-diverse-and-essential-roles-in-earths-ecosystem-june-2008-&catid=40:browse-all&Itemid=79 (July 27, 2011).

Damaging Light

My parents wedding photo hung in a relatively dark space for seventeen years in our New York home. When they moved to Florida, they put the framed image up in a prominent place in the dining room, hanging on the wall caddy-cornered to the large French doors and overlooking the lanai. Those doors let in large amounts of intense, tropical light. Within a few years, the color image became worn and faded, thanks to the bright Florida sun. My duplicate of the image remains colorful (if a bit worn from many moves around New England), sheltered from depleting beams of energy.

behind droppings, and encouraging the arrival of new, larger critters who feed on the smaller ones. Food and water supplies invite early intruders to enter your home. Warmth, cozy spaces, and a sustaining source of nutrition invites them to stay. To help avoid pest issues keep food out of the area where you store personal papers and make sure your building is properly sealed. Regularly maintain housecleaning on a fixed schedule to vacuum up particles upon which creatures may like to dine. Housecleaning can also eradicate any new eggs or nests.

Light—Causes materials to fade. Ideally, store originals away in appropriate enclosures and make copies for display and frequent handling.

Pollutants—Include gaseous vapors and particulates that can cause a variety of damage. Dust particulates can settle and abrade items or dirty them. Regular housekeeping measures such as vacuuming and dusting can reduce their potential damage. Use a HEPA vacuum—a regular vacuum just spews pollutants back into the room. Gaseous pollutants react and cause chemical damage. Avoid storing materials in garages, near the boiler, or near other places where chemical emissions may be high. Keep items in boxes for some protection against outside elements.

Water—Causes papers to warp, stick, discolor, and/or mold. Collections are best stored away from potential water-damaging situations. Keep personal papers out of basements and attics, where the humidity tends to be high, along with the potential for water accidents (i.e., flooding). Keep materials away from windows, skylights, air conditioners, hot water heaters, sinks, and ceilings with water pipes, which can leak. Raise boxes at least four inches above the floor, so if there is a small flood, materials will be above the water.

Figure 31. Water damage has caused discoloration, folding, and mold on these city records.

Beware of Odors

Old papers sometimes emanate strange and powerful smells. I first fell in love with old things when my fifth-grade teacher recognized my interest in history and suggested that I should ask my parents to take me to visit an old mansion that was up for sale in her neighborhood. I recall most strongly the smell of the grand library in the building and the memory of old books scattered everywhere. I have since associated the smell of mold with something precious. Though I wonder if my wonderful memory of the old building would be less intense had an odor not been present, having a mold problem is not a good thing. Regular housekeeping and air filtration can help keep spores from settling, and if a large outbreak occurs, such as the one that was likely occurring at the old mansion, it can be dangerous—one should contact a specialist.

Mold is a prime culprit of foul odors. Decomposing papers and plastics are another concern. If your boxes of personal papers smell, there is something wrong. Mild, unpleasant aromas arising from archival papers with no visible mold growth or obvious deterioration can often be remedied by reboxing and re-foldering items. If there is a strong odor, call a specialist. Materials smell when there is a problem, and smells are often signs of danger! The causes of odors may not only be dangerous to your materials, but they can be dangerous to your health as well. If you are unsure, get assistance.

Commonly Asked Questions about Preservation

Q. Is it a good idea to keep my personal papers in a bank vault?

Many people ask me about keeping materials in fireproof safes and bank vaults. Unfortunately, the environmental conditions in a bank vault are not necessarily conducive to the preservation of your items. Extreme changes in temperature and humidity have caused many individuals to lose paper items that they thought would be safe in the bank. For personal vaults and safes, be aware that the same problem may occur. Keep the safe in a room with a stable environment. Check it periodically for deterioration.

Q. Are my framed photos safe?

It is best to place your photographs and artwork in a window mat hinged to backing board, both made of buffered mat board. The window prevents the image from sticking to the glass if there are issues with humidity. It is best to make copies rather than displaying originals if you can. Scan and store originals. Prints can be framed, collaged, or otherwise used without fear that your original will be harmed. If for some reason you want to display an original, make sure that all the mat board and backing used in the process are acid- and lignin-free. Keep your framed images out of direct sunlight and bright spaces. For extra protection, use UV-filtering glass or acrylic to help block harmful rays.

Q. How can I tell if the supplies I've already used are safe for my materials?

There are a couple of ways you can learn whether the materials you are using are safe. First, if the storage supplies have an odor, get rid of them. You can be confident that they are not safe. For paper supplies, use a pH-testing pen, which you can purchase from a reputable archives supplier. An ink mark made by this pen changes color based on the acidity of the item. If you are unsure about the quality of the storage material, get rid of it. It is better to be safe than sorry with your unique family materials.

Q. Can I store my photographs in plastic sleeves?

Avoid plastics with PVC. Polyester, polyethylene, and polypropylene sleeves without surface coatings and plasticizers are acceptable. Look for an indication that the product has passed the Photographic Activity Test (PAT) to determine if they have chemical alterations, additives, or coatings that might be harmful to photographic materials. I always recommend buying materials from a reputable supplier just to be on the safe side.

Q. Is laminating my valuable materials a good idea?

The number-one tenet of preservation is never do anything that is irreversible. We once thought that lamination was a good idea. When items began to yellow in the laminating plastic and/or the plastics began to disintegrate, we could not easily remove the lamination materials. Preferable to lamination, we now use various types of PVC-free, polyester, polyethylene, or polypropylene plastic sleeves that can be easily removed by sliding materials out. They keep fingerprints off our cherished items without causing other kinds of damage. These sleeves are open-ended on at least one side to allow for better air flow and off-gassing of volatile chemicals. (In other words, give the chemicals that can hurt your materials a way to move from your cherished items.)

Q. How do I eliminate mold from my items?

Mold can pose a significant risk to personal health as well as collections, so great care is required. If the mold is extensive and active (powdery spores), it is best to call in a conservator. Consider whether the items are worth saving—even after treatment, spores may reactivate if exposed to warm humidity in the future. Unless you are susceptible to mold, you may be able to handle small mold problems on your own, including cases where a box of records has been subjected to a small basement flood and has been immediately removed. Wear a HEPA mask that filters out fine particulates and gloves that keep harmful materials off of your skin. Dry materials fully. Take the items outdoors and carefully brush the mold spores off of the surface. Once you're done, wash your hands, tools, and clothing. Find a better storage space, one that is dry, to avoid a repeat.

Q. How do I eliminate the musty smell from my items?

Make sure that what you have is just a mold smell and not active mold, which can be a health hazard. If in doubt, ask an expert. To eliminate the smell of mold, consider Starbrite mildew control bags, which are available online through Amazon and other dealers. To eliminate the smell of mold from archival material using common household items, create a chamber using trash cans. Place a small can containing your archival material into a larger can. Place baking soda or unscented kitty litter in the large can (away from your items). Cover the larger can with its lid. Leave materials in for a few days and check periodically. The odor-absorbing material—the kitty litter or baking soda—should pull away smells over time.

Q. Will scanning harm my materials?

"Preservation copies" or display copies of original items can be easily made by scanning or by taking photographs of originals. The one-time flash of light will not have negative effects on items, though taking many pictures could. Many museums ask visitors to refrain from taking photographs primarily for this reason (though intellectual property issues might be considered, too). Scanning is often the easiest way to duplicate materials that are not brittle or oversized, whereas photography is preferred for brittle or oversized archives and for artifacts. Setting a tripod up with a camera, using a photo cube to avoid reflections, and shooting down at manuscripts is the best way to obtain a good photographic image of them. Do not push down on bindings of journals and books to get a good scan. To avoid damage, try photographing materials, or send treasured or brittle items to a professional photographer who specializes in restoration to make a good copy.

Q. Do I need to wear gloves when handling old materials?

Oils from our fingers can be harmful to all materials but are most harmful to the emulsion on photographs. Our finger oils can leave great big fingerprints that eat away at the image over time. Tests have identified sodium chloride as the active ingredient in sweat, the "oil" on your fingers that can lead to staining on archival materials. Many archivists wear gloves when working with any type of archival documents to reduce contamination. This is a personal choice with your home materials. I wear gloves when handling photographs because this medium is particularly susceptible to finger oils, but I find gloves to be generally awkward.

For example, they make page-turning difficult. Always wash hands before touching documents to eliminate dirt and reduce oils that can harm items. Do not touch your face or hair while working on archival materials.

Q. Can I use staples and paper clips on my personal papers?

It is best, whenever possible, to remove these unnecessary fasteners from the collection. Gently pull apart paper clips, lifting from the front and back, to avoid tearing documents. Use a microspatula (available from archival suppliers) to lift out staples. Do not use the common staple removers with "teeth" that can easily tear your papers. If it is necessary to keep items separated from other materials in the collection for organizational purposes using a smaller grouping than the folder level, fold a piece of acid-free paper in half and use as an envelope for items.

Q. How can I save papers that have gotten wet?

Paper is fragile when wet, so handle with care. Dry out wet individual sheets by placing them on a hard surface with blotter paper beneath. If you do not have blotter paper, use unprinted newsprint. Tablets can be purchased from an art supply store. If the paper is very wet, blot the moisture with paper towels. When pages are nearly dry, place them under a flat surface such as a baking sheet in a stack under weight to flatten—a nice pile of heavy books or bricks can do the trick for weight. Some cockling (warping of pages) is inevitable. Coated paper— the shiny paper found in magazines—poses a greater threat because the coatings can fuse, causing the pages to stick. In this case, every page needs to be interleaved. If you do not have time to do this, freeze them and defrost. Interleave and dry materials when you have more time. Pages in books with sturdy bindings can be fanned open. Close them and place under weights when almost dry.

Leave fans running to circulate air so that mold is less likely to develop. If there is water damage in a room where personal papers are stored, make sure materials are removed from the area to a place where humidity levels are lower. Use dehumidifiers when necessary. If your materials have gotten wet and it is not possible to quickly dry them, put them in a plastic baggy and place them in a freezer until they can be properly treated. This will help prevent an outbreak of mold. Freezing will not kill the mold, but it will prevent it from spreading while it remains in frozen storage. Do not leave unfrozen materials in bags: This can exacerbate the problem, creating a warm microclimate conducive to further mold growth. Call a conservator for assistance.[47]

Q. How do I remove photos from magnetic albums?

When photos are stuck to your old album pages, try gently using a microspatula or dental floss to wiggle under the image and lift it off. If there are no images on the other side, a second resort is sometimes to use a hair dryer set on low to warm the back of the page to melt the glue a bit; the image can then be released from the page. Never heat the page too long, use a high setting, or heat the emulsion side of the image. Proceed with caution with any of these steps or risk damaging your original!

Q. Can I safely clean my personal papers?

Papers can be gently blown with air using a brush blower or brushed with a specially designed soft-haired brush to remove loose dirt. For adhered grime, one may be able to use a special dry-cleaning sponge that can gently rub away dirt. These are sold through reputable archives supply companies. Be extremely gentle, and do not use this method on pencil, charcoal, and other nonbinding marks that are integral elements of your documents. These marks will be removed along with dirt. Keep in mind that not everything needs to be cleaned. Only use this method when you fear dirt will harm the item and when you are sure that cleaning will not cause additional harm. As with all preservation processes, consult a specialist if you are unsure.

Q. Are archives supplies expensive?

If you are concerned about costs (because photographic supplies for preservation can be costly), consider what is the least that can be done for the greatest value. Removing primary enclosures that touch your materials directly should be a priority, but replacing these items with the "perfect" primary enclosure is often

---

[47] "Emergency Drying Procedures for Water-Damaged Collections," *Library of Congress Preservation,* www.loc.gov/preservation/care/dry.html (July 27, 2011).

not as important. If you can afford nothing else, remove damaging enclosures and place items in preservation-safe folders and boxes. Try to budget for materials that better suit your materials' particular needs. For example, buy the perfect-sized boxes over time. Purchase appropriate plastic sleeves and envelopes down the road if you cannot do that now.

Evaluating your use of your materials can help lower supply costs. Photo supplies are among the costliest. Consider boxing some items and placing only your favorites in albums. Individual photographs can be stored in boxes or albums, whatever works best for your budget and viewing pleasure. I keep images I want to see often in an album. I place images that I view less often in archival boxes. I allow my young daughter to look through many of the images, so many of the boxed ones are kept in plastic enclosures that passed PAT to keep off fingerprints, but this does add to the storage expense and isn't necessary if you are careful to hold images by the edge.

Mental and Writing Exercises for Preservation

1. Make a list of five to ten items among your materials that have preservation issues that concern you. Put asterisks next to the materials that seem to be in the most danger. Make these a priority as you work to improve the conditions of your collection.

2. Consider the place(s) where you currently store your archives. Do they adhere to appropriate preservation standards in terms of keeping materials free from excessive climate fluctuations, lights, pests, water, and pollutants?

3. Consider your storage materials. Make a prioritized list of improvements that you can make over time. Include such things as reboxing, re-foldering, adding interleaving papers, etc.

4. Identify the ephemera in your collection. Is the material yellowing or otherwise deteriorating faster than other materials in your collection? Make a list of five ways that you can slow this process and/or save the information in the materials.

5. Identify an item that you know can be improved by using alternate storage, but that you do not want to change. (Use my baby book on page 137 as a model.) Is there anything you can do to make the situation better?

6. Note any items or groups of papers that have preservation issues requiring conservation. Decide if these materials are valuable enough to you to visit a conservator.

7. Note your current method of storage for your photographs. Is there anything about it that you would change based on the information in this chapter?

8. Make a list of records you would try to grab in an emergency.

Chapter Six:
Ideas for Recording
Unrecorded History

Filling In Your Personal Narrative

"View your documents as a collection and see if they put together a story about your life." Do you remember that sentence and these questions from Chapter Two?

"Do [your documents] show your personal point of view? Do they effectively tell what is important to you? Do they show how you function from day-to-day? Do they highlight your achievements?"

The things that are important to you should find their way into your personal documentation. Once you have organized, described, and preserved what is recorded, you should have a good idea of what is missing from your personal narrative. Now is the time to fill in the gaps to make sure the questions I've posed above are answered.

Documenting the Unrecorded

This chapter gives you ideas for ways to record the vital parts of your story that are not yet written or otherwise recorded. The sections of this book on personal narrative and archival appraisal identified the types of existing materials that help us build personal and community stories when gathered together. Through the discussions in this book, you have at least started to think about what is important to document in your life and have probably given some thought to what stories are not being recorded and passed on to others. Now you can work to ensure that your most important memories are captured. I aim to present you with a number of options for documenting that will allow you to relive events and communicate your experiences to others, using methods that suit the stories you have to convey and that suit your personality.

Consider the anecdotes that are passed on informally through family stories or traditions. Review the objects in your home that have meaning that only you would know about. Think about the quirky habits your family develops over time that represent your unique personal culture. Identify family members' memorable verbal expressions or unique gestures. Begin thinking about how you can record these things and attach meaning to them so that they can be conveyed to future generations.

For example, when my daughter was a baby, she would crinkle her nose, narrow her eyes, and scrunch her lips when sitting at the dinner table until someone looked at her and laughed. This was our first sign that she has a wonderful sense of humor. I forgot about her funny way for a while until a few years after discontinuing her silly faces, she crinkled her nose at the table to express displeasure. I said to my husband, "Hey! Remember that funny face she did all the time?" We now regularly try to get her to duplicate the baby face, but she does not remember it, and it is never quite right. I need to see if we caught it on video. Otherwise, we will resort to reminiscing about it, and the exact facial expression, like so many bits of personal family lore, will be lost to time.

I have peppered orphan images throughout this book that have lost meaning due to unrecorded information. The image at the beginning of this chapter is a good example of an undocumented story. Students pose for a group picture at some kind of celebratory event. In front of them is a sign that says "No Hunting." The sign is odd and seemingly out of place here. I will wonder forever what it means and what the story behind it is. I wish someone had labeled this image to

Unrecorded Quirks and Idiosyncrasies

What really makes me...well, me? And what makes you...you? I have different genetics—a different family tree. I also live differently. Perhaps I live in a different place and in a different kind of house. I likely have different hobbies and a different job than you do...but there are other people in similar categories. There are probably even New Hampshire archivists living in modern colonial homes who spend the majority of their days in front of a computer. To me, the defining aspects of me are the quirks that generally only those closest to me know. For example, all of the people close to me (and soon you will) know that Snoopy is one of my favorite things in the world. Although people currently like to gift to me all things Snoopy, my grandchildren just may wonder one day why an old box of Snoopy figurines sits in the back corner of my daughter's closet. Perhaps someone should tell them (i.e., I should record somewhere) that I decorated my house with a cartoon character just so that I could run into it during the day because he made me smile.

Food Culture

Food is an important part of our culture, identity, and personal narratives. A food biography can tell us much about a person, from one's ethnic background to maybe even one's health. *Write Your Own Food Biography: My Life in Ten Dishes* (see footnote on the next page) reminds us that food "has an incredible power to evoke the past; to remind us of special occasions, disasters and triumphs, and those long gone." A colleague and I had great fun listing the ten foods that we felt most influenced us and the memories that we associated with them. With very different backgrounds, our informal inventory of the cuisine of our lives was quite diverse. However, the memories for both of us were tied to loved ones and special times in our lives.

tell me.

Following principles of appraisal, documenting communities, and ideas about developing narrative, individuals should consider the aspects of their lives that deserve documenting. Use objects and photos as launching points for conveying stories. Take note of times you laugh at the things your children do and the idiosyncrasies you spot in your spouse. Think about what you will want to remember when you grow old. Are you taking it all in? Are you recording what is most important to you?

Return to the timeline of the important events that have occurred in your life that I discussed in Chapter Two. If you have not created a timeline, now may be a good time to do so. List the documentation that you have that relates to the topics you outline; then list what needs further exploration. For events with no documentation, consider your options for creating some using the ideas in this chapter.

Realistically, most of us will not create a full historical record of our life, nor is it necessary to do so. One can concentrate on creating a well-rounded view of one's life without detail for every event. Become aware of what you are documenting and what you are not documenting. Determine what important aspects of your life and personality that you want to preserve and/or share are missing from your personal papers. Make efforts to provide a broad overview of your life, then hone in on details if you have the time or inclination.

Most of us make records of specific events such as holidays, achievements, birthdays, new homes, trips, etc. We are trained to habitually grab the camera to make permanent note of certain circumstances. Some other events in our lives have official paperwork associated with them that requires us to fill in forms or to otherwise write information. However, some of the most defining aspects of our lives do not require or encourage automatic documentation—these are the times we need to consider more carefully.

We may get too busy to ensure that memories are written down, that photos are taken, or that videos are recorded. In other cases, we do not thoroughly consider what aspects of our lives are worth recording for posterity. After reading this far into this book, you should realize the value of paying attention to those important lifetime moments that are desirable to record. This awareness can propel us to make the memories of them into something tangible. Recording unwritten history provides us with a unique opportunity to use our creativity and directly inject our personality into that which we create.[48]

In some cases, there is recorded information related to an idea, but the recorded information is incomplete. An individual image of a place may raise

Travel Memories

Listed below are certain elements that you may want to include in a vacation journal. Journals are a great way to help you record and remember your adventures. Journal entries do not need to be long. Use your journal to record what is important to you, or record memories on a blog. Make it a pleasurable experience. Include short entries, long descriptions, even doodles. Include the date and consider incorporating the following: weather, list of day's activities, list of who was there, unusual or favorite foods eaten, favorite memory of the day, something learned, a souvenir found, or why you would like to go back to this place. For handwritten journals, the following companies provide varied product options:

- Moleskine: www.moleskineus.com
- Eccolo: www.eccololtd.com
- Piccadilly: www.piccadillyinc.com
- Mead: bit.ly/9wpoRF

---

[48] In the textbox on the previous page, food culture is presented as an important piece of unwritten history. For more information, see Jill Dupleix and Terry Durack, "Write Your Own Food Biography: My Life in Ten Dishes," www.theage.com.au/entertainment/blogs/table-talk/write-your-own-food-biography-my-life-in-10-dishes/20100729-10xrd.html (July 27, 2011).

more questions than it answers. Who is included in the photograph? What place is depicted? Making truly reflective collections involves ensuring that the tangible documentation is as complete as we can make it, revealing various aspects of a subject, perhaps in different formats, and perhaps with diverse viewpoints. For example, a memory of Thanksgiving might include: photos of the meal, a list of people attending, a description of decorations and heirlooms used on the table, a menu and recipes, or a written account of the day's activities (perhaps in a diary or separate log, and maybe even a few accounts written by different people). One might even go so far as to take video recordings to capture voices and mannerisms.

Figure 32. When I was young, my mother (pictured on the lower right) made a special trip by herself to travel "all the way" to British Columbia for her brother's wedding. I can imagine people moving into place to pose for this image. I can almost hear the happy people laughing. How could another form of documentation round out the story and provide the details I can only imagine? A home movie or a diary written by my aunt or uncle that describes their wedding day would be nice. Even a picture of the photographer as he was taking this picture could help us better understand the context of this image.

Identifying What Aspects of ME Are Unrecorded

Let's examine a "typical" morning in the suburban United States. A family of four awakens. The kids are shuffled off to school. The parents have some coffee and drive to work. The kids work in school on assignments, create in art class, and play at recess. The parents attend meetings, work on assignments, and take a morning coffee break. What aspects of the morning are being recorded and what aspects are not? Does the information that is being automatically generated in the form of school papers, meeting minutes, class artwork, and typed files provide enough information for us to understand a typical American morning? Is attending a meeting more documentation-worthy than regular mornings of chitchat around a coffee at break time? Is art class where I created something tangible more interesting to recall than recess?

The challenge of identifying what aspects of me are unrecorded and what aspects are memory-worthy is twofold. First, it is difficult to consider every moment of my life trapped in my brain and to highlight

Blah, Blah, Blogging

A blog is a website on which one regularly posts information. It can be a news site or serve as a sort of online newsletter. Many times it functions as a personal journal, allowing the writer to get across his point of view and relate his experiences to others. A blog usually encourages comments to the author's postings. WordPress and Blogger are currently the two most popular blogging platforms. Below are two entertaining blogs that use a diary-like writing style.

www.skittlesplace.net—Barb openly writes about her life struggles. I think this blog demonstrates a cathartic approach to blogging.

nataliemurray.blogspot.com—Diary of a Girl Abroad features beautiful photos, bulleted lists, and fun, short posts that give us a quick peek into the author's head.

There are so many wonderful blogs out there. It is fun to just "Google" and explore them.

Home Journaling

In addition to journaling about day-to-day activities, you can also create special journals about things in life that you may wish to pay more attention to or to highlight. A home journal is one way to do this. Record the significant things that happen to your home—home improvements, out-of-town visitors, regular celebrations that make use of your space. Think of this journal as a documentation of your place, as if your home is another character within your community. In the past, people kept guest books that visitors would sign when they entered the parlor. They would also leave calling cards to mark their visit. These actions significantly celebrated the home as one's personal space and one's willingness to share it with friends and neighbors.

the important parts. Second, it is challenging to make sure that we give equal weight to equal events. Returning to our example, my daughter has come home from school every day for the past six weeks with a spring in her step. She runs off the bus to tell me what she learned to do on the monkey bars during the day. A close friend of hers formed a "monkey bar club." To my daughter, at this particular moment in her life, monkey bars are the most important thing in the world. She asks me if I liked the monkey bars when I was young. Truthfully, I don't really remember if I did. I want to remember, but the knowledge of my recess preference at the age of seven is lost to time. I feel like I'm missing something by lacking that knowledge. I am missing a certain understanding of my childhood self, and I am missing a mother-daughter (community) bonding opportunity.

Figure 33. Calling cards were once left in bowls on the front hall table to mark the occasion of a guest's visit. Perhaps you want to renew this old tradition or consider replacing this method with a guest book, home journal, or another clever documentation method of your choosing to celebrate home and friendship.

Discover the Best Formats for Your Stories

Although it is a challenge to identify the aspects of our lives that are important to highlight, it can be equally tricky to find appropriate ways to record those worthwhile lifetime moments. The format that documentation will take is limited only by our imaginations. Barring preservation concerns, there is no right or wrong way to record that which is important to us. From diaries and paper scrapbooks to YouTube videos and digitized photo albums, the means we use to document and convey an individual story can be tailored to our personal preferences and whims.

Some means may seem more suitable to particular situations. For example, if we want to capture family stories, oral histories are an ideal way to record and impart the ideas of many people with varied viewpoints. Or for example, if we want to capture a sense of place, creating a video or a photo essay will stand as a visual representation that allows viewers to see that area for themselves.

My Coney Island Memories—Creating Local Communities Online

Your digital documentation does not need to be complicated. I stumbled across a wonderful site called My Coney Island Memories while doing research about a photo that I picked up online at Etsy.com. (I have begun collecting photographs and ephemera to help me illustrate my writing and presentations, and most of the illustrations in this book come from my personal collections.) My Coney Island Memories is simple: It starts with an individual's early childhood memories of a special place. It runs for a few pages and incorporates ephemera and photographs illustrating the author's remarks. It reads like an online personal diary and is supplemented by a page of transcribed e-mails that were sent to the author by other people who had memories of Coney Island. The creator of the page struck a chord and developed an online community of former Coney Island visitors and residents who could reach each other through this fabulous medium.

(www.myconeyislandmemories.com)

How are you recording that which is important to you? Do you always run first for the video camera? (I tend to prefer still images over all else.) And how do you decide when to begin recording? We generally move into documentary mode for major events. We pull out the camera for holidays and birthdays. We make movies of baby's first steps. What about all the times in between? You can make telling your story a part of your regular routine without too much effort. Whether you have a way with words, are more of a visual person, or enjoy working with numbers, you can find a documentation method that is an easy fit for your personality. Creating a record of your life has value, and the method by which you choose to create that record can have special meaning if you imbue it with your personality. The way you choose to tell your story can and should be a reflection of who you are and what is important to you. Be creative. Do what you like. Feed your talents, and documentation work will come easily to you. Do not try to keep a long journal if you are not a writer. Do not try to record the weather every day if you are not meticulous. Do not create a photo scrapbook if it is a chore. In other words, when creating documentation, do not use a method that you think you *should* do—do what you *want* to do. The method is not the content. There is more than one way to convey a narrative. The way you choose to tell your story is just the shell. It is what the shell contains that is important.

Figure 34. This image shows people having their photo taken at one of the many streetside studios that used props such as this car and other objects such as steeplechase horses. The Coney Island History Project has other examples of tourist pictures through its Flickr photo stream. See the website with oral histories of Coney Island memories at www.coneyislandhistory.org/index.php.

Journaling

Keeping a journal is a good way to document what is important to us. Diary writing is not for everyone. However, there are many who think that they do not want to take the time to keep a lengthy journal, but they are willing to write about themselves in another way. Diary writing does not have to be long or tedious. In fact, only about a century ago, it was common for many people to keep short journals that described the weather and maybe gave one or two sentences about daily activities. These items provide much insight into the contemporary lives of the times. Diary entries can be as long (or as short) as you want to make them. They can also be written every day or can be sporadic. I tend to be a crisis/contented diary writer. I will run up to my room and write at times when I am particularly upset to help me work out my thoughts. I will also write when I am very calm and want to note what has brought me to this special place of happiness. I do not often write during in-between times, which is to say most of the time. I could put my diary down for months. I think I have even put it down for years, but I always come back to it at some point. I leaf through my entries at times and sometimes do "retrospectives" where I will write an entry that fills gaps that my previous entries did not cover, but I do not always do this.

Annual Reflection

Over tea with a neighbor, I chatted about the difficulty of keeping up with the album that I maintain for my daughter. Every few months I would print out my favorite digital pictures and place them in an album, but in year seven I fell completely out of step with my routine. When December had rolled around, I realized I had not done anything with the photographs I took all that year. My friend explained her method for keeping up with the memories. Every year, she and her husband write a letter to their daughter that gives a summary of the events of that year. It includes things she liked and how her personality was growing. They keep each letter in a special box that they plan to give her when she's older, perhaps when she turns sixteen. I could not think of a nicer or simpler way to record a childhood and ensure that the memories are preserved. An album does not have to be the only or best way to convey what is important to us.

Ideas for Short and Sweet Journals

- Gourmands—List what was served at memorable events and what you liked best.
- Parents of kids in sports—List games, scores, and memorable moments at each game.
- Hobbyists/builders—List projects, your reasons for pursuing each, what you learn from the experience, and what you do with each creation when it is complete.
- Genealogists—List your visits to particular research centers and write what impressed you most about your experience there.
- Museum-goers—List museums you frequent and your favorite objects at various institutions.
- Gardeners—List what you plant and when. Tour your garden each month and note how things are growing.
- Book lovers—List books you've read and describe what you liked or did not like about them.
- Skiers—List each day on the slopes, the temperature, and your most memorable snowy moments.

Documentation opportunities are endless, but each journal entry need not take a long time.

Writing is not the only way to create narrative of that which is important to us. Many people do not like to "write" but may wish to consider making journal lists that document the facts of the day. As a little girl, I often filled notebooks with lists that began "My favorite things are…" or "The cutest boys are…." Use this concept to create a format for an event: "The most memorable moments of the day were…" or "I had to laugh when…," You can even use this format to focus on one aspect of an event that is most meaningful to you. Or create individual journals for special things in your life, such as hobbies and other passions.

Short and sweet journal entries may even jar memories that encourage you to keep writing. Tailor your lists to the event. There is nothing wrong with focusing on one thing if the whole process of creating documentation from nothing is overwhelming to you. A list is not only better than nothing: It can be a key to understanding what is important to you and your family for future generations. You may even consider creating a "mind map," which is a nonlinear, visual way of organizing thoughts.[49]

However, if you do like to write, you are probably journaling already. Your journal may naturally include the happenings of your days and your feelings about a wide range of topics. If you fall into the "I like to write" category, take a look at what you are producing. Are there any valuable aspects of you that you are neglecting? Do your journals give a well-rounded view of your life? Does your writing fully describe the people and locations around you? Do you think you can be more descriptive?

Documenting the Mundane

My daughter walks in from school every day and yells, "I'm home!"

When we were kids, my brother used to wander around the house singing to himself. (And it's a family trait that has been passed from him to my daughter somehow.)

My sister once spent her days sitting in trees trying to catch butterflies.

All of these things seem(ed) very ordinary, but they are the unique, mundane aspects of my life that have helped me form special connections with loved ones.

What individual habits are so a part of your life that they are likely to be easily overlooked in documentation efforts? How can you capture these moments so you remember them for posterity? Make a list of what happens to you today that regularly occurs in your life. Ask other family members about past habits and their memories of them.

---

[49] See more on Mind Mapping from its creator at www.thinkbuzan.com/us/articles/view/how-to-create-a-mind-map.

Figure 35 An avid gardener, I kept track of the plantings and goings-on in my first garden in the yard of my former home.

Storytelling Project: StoryCorps

StoryCorps is one of the largest oral history projects in the world. Its mission "is to provide Americans of all backgrounds and beliefs with the opportunity to record, share, and preserve the stories of our lives. Since 2003, StoryCorps has collected and archived more than 30,000 interviews from more than 60,000 participants." Interviews are added to the collections at the American Folklife Center at the Library of Congress and are shared regularly through National Public Radio. This unique project raises awareness about the value of personal stories and the need for creative ways to document them. StoryCorps allows citizens to see a large-scale oral history project in action. People can use their example to enhance their personal documentation efforts, recording family stories that may before have received little attention. These efforts can benefit their relatives, communities, and future generations.

www.storycorps.org

Oral History

Creating an oral history is an extremely valuable way to record previously unrecorded memories and history. Oral history involves interviewing people about their personal experiences and recording them for posterity. Many repositories, such as historical societies, museums, and other cultural heritage institutions, conduct formal oral histories to fill gaps in community documentation. For example, they may decide to interview octogenarians in town about times few people remember. They may interview veterans about experiences to better highlight how the community was affected by war. A community may decide to interview people who lived through certain events of local importance or highlight a national event to see how it impacted the town. As with any documentation project, the possibilities are endless. [50]

People conduct oral histories professionally, creating well-defined projects to supplement important stories already housed in repositories. Family history is just as important to record. The simplest oral history projects can

Oral Recordings

The community of Waltham, Massachusetts, pursued a major documentation project in the 1980s that centered on oral history. The city encouraged members of communities to step forward and celebrate their ethnicity through a series of parties for each immigrant group represented in town. People were also encouraged to share documents and photographs for the creation of a book called *Waltham Rediscovered* about the growth of Waltham and its immigrant populations. These documents and photographs served as launching points for storytelling and reminiscing. The project was enthusiastically received, and much history was collected. Taped recordings of diverse local residents served as research for the book, were transcribed, and were later donated to the Waltham Public Library during my tenure as their archivist in the mid-1990s. The *Waltham Rediscovered Collection* is a valuable community resource that holds the stories of Waltham and its resident families.

[50] Much has been written about conducting oral histories. The Center for the Study of History and Memory at Indiana University, Bloomington, provides good advice on its "Oral History Techniques: How to Organize and Conduct Oral History Interviews" Web page (www.indiana.edu/~cshm/techniques.html).

involve grandkids questioning grandparents about their childhoods.

Encouraging kids to question boosts an interest in history and serves as a wonderful bonding experience. The creation of valuable family documentation that can be saved for generations is a bonus. People have said to me many times that they wish they asked their parents questions while they were still around or while their parents had the faculties to answer. Because oral history is not complicated, time-consuming, or expensive, you can arrange interviews immediately. Overcome any reticence from those you wish to question by explaining why you want to hear their stories and how meaningful they are to you.

Family reunions and holidays where the whole family is gathered are perfect times for setting up interviews. If you do not have a "perfect" occasion, create your own opportunity. It is possible to conduct interviews by phone or through the computer. You can even be creative and write letters back and forth to conduct "interviews."

Another bonus to oral history is that you can use the occasion to encourage relatives to dig out pictures that will jar memories. Identify people in the photos and label them! Old mementos, letters, and other saved materials can serve as a starting point for questions, and oral history can morph into a diverse documentation project if you want it to.

Visual Media

For those who are more visual, photographs made into collages, scrapbooks, slideshows, and websites might be a preferable way to create documentation of events. Many online photo sites make this type of work easy for you. One type of documentation that is gaining popularity and is getting easier to complete is a photo book. You may upload your images to a website and arrange them in a format of your choosing, or you may pick a prearranged format and place your images where you desire. You may even ask the site to do the arranging for you. Online photo-share sites such as Kodak Gallery, Picaboo, Pixagogo, Shutterfly, SmugMug, and Webshots prompt you for captions and provide artful backgrounds and dynamic arrangement options.

Albums and scrapbooks can, of course, still be done the "old-fashioned" way. Be sure to pick photo-safe materials as described in the "Preservation" chapter. Be sure to label your visual creations to include names, dates, and places pictured. Once again, your ideas for documenting the undocumented can be creative. Do not feel tied to a specific way of doing things. Last year, for example, I did not have the time to cull digital photos every month for printing and adding to my daughter's album as I usually do. Instead, I picked through the photos in December with certain important events in mind (her birthday, my brother's wedding where she was a flower girl, first-grade field day, Halloween, etc.) and created a

Creating a Collage

A friend recently told me about a collage she made and brought to an event to celebrate the life of a deceased loved one. She grew concerned after she shared the collage with family members that it would get stuffed behind a bureau or otherwise stored and forgotten. She decided to take the photos she used and the captions she wrote to memorialize her relative and arrange them into a published scrapbook through an online photo service. She is conscious of the formatting and is combining words and text to create something permanent and memorable to give to her family.

A Sense of Place: Memories of Home

My parents moved from the town where I was raised when I graduated from high school. To commemorate the event and the passing of my childhood, I created a photo essay of our home for a final project in my senior AP art class. I photographed the street sign. I captured our landscape. I took an image of each room. I even managed to sneak into my sister's messy room to make sure the memory of her unmade bed was recorded for posterity. This was my teenage way of preserving my identity and demonstrating my community connection. The essay stands as a testament to my point of view. (For example, I'm sure my sister would have made the bed had she done the project.) Any documentation project on which you embark will contain a little bit of you. Aim for diversity and at least a little bit of objectivity (perhaps even despite some sibling rivalry).

book online that shows my daughter's year in summary. I had the book made into a small twenty-page remembrance album that I printed for myself for a holiday present.

Similarly, during her short school career, each year my daughter has been assigned to do a personal collage by her teachers. She has picked out the images that she thinks best represent her, has incorporated meaningful words, and has created three collages of her life. It is interesting to see how every year changes, while some things stay the same. Mommy and Daddy are always on there, and so is her best friend, while the favorite toy has sometimes been included and the most memorable event is always different. This project does not need to be one just for a child. Consider what matters to you in a particular year and make your collage. The one I made in my twenties would certainly be different from the one I make now.

If all you can do is a yearly evaluation, consider it valuable for filling at least a small part of your documentation gap. If you only feel creative once a year, choose a project that is fun for you and the family to do together. Pay attention to the things you see that you want preserved forever and record them appropriately—so others can see the world through your eyes.

Sense of Place

The backdrop to your personal story provides a valuable bit of information toward the understanding of your personal history, but it is one of those intangible elements that you will likely need to consciously convey and incorporate into your documentation efforts. A setting can influence us and the events around us in poignant ways. "Who am I?" has been influenced by the places I have lived.

For example, I grew up in a suburban environment, in a town about 45 minutes outside of New York City. I could walk to school and to the grocery store. Wildlife consisted of birds, bugs, and an occasional raccoon in the garbage. Sidewalks were the norm, and my cul-de-sac enabled me to learn to ride my bike without fear of being hit by a car. I now live in a more rural suburban environment. I need a vehicle to get almost anywhere. The hills are too big for easily learning to ride a bike. I have had deer, fox, and fisher cats in my yard. Frogs keep me up at night instead of traffic, and friends have told me that there is a bear in the neighborhood. My formative years were certainly different from my daughter's early years, and her sense of self has a distinctly New Hampshire tinge to it. When we visit a city, she is struck by all the people and buildings, noting them as distinctly different from her norm.

"Hey Buddy, Where You from?" (Said with a New York Accent)

Moving to another place can be a shock to one's sensibilities. After 22 years in New England, I still call their "jimmies" "sprinkles," but in college I immediately rid myself of the telltale accent that revealed me as a New Yorker. Today, I am still mesmerized by the frozen brooks that surround me, and the mountains that are only miles from my home. They will always have a bit of an "otherness" to me. They were not my norm growing up, and now I think I appreciate them more than my friends who grew up here. My brain remembers fast-paced New York style, while life around me sometimes runs at more of a country pace. And although I appreciate my new place, I sometimes still find my sensibilities at odds with the surroundings. My early childhood family photos are set more in asphalt, while my middle-aged images are surrounded by trees, creating a dichotomy to my life story that needs a little explaining.

Figure 36. I asked my mother to send me photos of her and Dad from their childhoods that demonstrate a sense of place. Their city upbringings are evident in these images. Mom stands with her little brother in a carriage. Dad is the little boy on the lower left in the other image.

The place from which we come gives us shared memories with other community members.[51] The place may also deeply impact us so that our "otherness" is obvious to others. Transmitting remembrances about our spaces is vital toward helping others understand us. One who lives in the inner city will have a very different perspective than one who lives in the country. A person of a particular nationality will also have alternate views from someone from another place. Explaining these differences is vital toward promoting harmony among diverse groups and can help us better understand ourselves and each other.

Try to capture your environment in your documentation work. Use visual tools to relay your setting to others. Describe what makes the place or places you have lived unique. Try to convey how your sense of place has impacted you. Use sense of place as a thread through your other documentation work, or focus exclusively on it by describing the setting directly. To convey your sense of place, think about the location itself. Consider the buildings, natural elements, and infrastructure that you recognize as your own. Also mull over the cultural environment that your residence has that makes it unique. What characteristics of the community reflect its uniqueness? What language, ideas, history, and recurring events are distinctive elements of this place?

---

[51] For more on "sense of place," please see Robert Archibald's *A Place to Remember: Using History to Build Community* (Lanham, MD: AltaMira Press, 1999).

Intangible Heritage

There are many aspects of culture that do not automatically generate documentation. Languages, food, dance, music, storytelling, play-acting, medicine, and craft-making are some of the cultural elements we describe as "intangible heritage." To ensure that these aspects of culture are kept alive, groups need to consciously relate information that continues traditions and passes on the legacy of activity. Through oral transmission and demonstration, practitioners give their knowledge to newer generations. The keepers of such knowledge often do not think to record it in the event those living with proficiency in a certain area are not able to transfer it to their community in traditional ways. Many cultural heritage professionals are working to find ways to record intangible heritage. [52]

Intangible heritage dies more often than we would like to think. Recipes go unrecorded. People adopt new speaking habits and do not value older means of communication. Societies come up with innovative ways of making things and let go of the old methods. Throughout our history, we have lost "secret" ingredients to make fabulous dishes, have forgotten languages of our ancestors, and have abandoned tried-and-true "old-fashioned" ways of constructing things in favor of mass-production. Over time, those who had knowledge of former ways pass away. New generations sometimes find that they need to

Intangible Heritage Lists

UNESCO maintains the Intergovernmental Committee for the Safeguarding of Intangible Cultural Heritage to identify and support those aspects of culture that are not easily documented. The following are some of the recent international heritage expressions and practices that they have added to their Intangible Heritage Lists. It is provided to show the diversity of these traditions:

- Ojkanje singing—Croatia
- Aalst carnival—Belgium
- Chhau dance—India
- Falconry—multinational
- Human towers—Spain
- Carpet-weaving—Iran
- Cross-stones art—Armenia
- Peking opera—China
- Oil-wrestling festival—Turkey

---

[52] UNESCO Heritage Lists 2010 (www.unesco.org/culture/ich/index.php?lg=en&pg=00011).

Preserving Heritage

An American friend of mine married a Tibetan man who was living in exile in Dharamsala, India. Many Tibetans were displaced from their homeland and struggle to keep their culture alive outside of the geographic region in which they and/or their ancestors were born. My friend and her husband now have a little boy. They are making a concerted effort to pass on Tibetan traditions. This includes teaching their son the Tibetan language, even though it is not commonly used in the New England city where he now lives. Passing on intangible heritage can be difficult, but it often represents and keeps intact a vital part of our identity. Intangible heritage ties us strongly to the past, our ancestors, and our humanity. It can fuel our sense of survival and secure us to something larger than ourselves.

rediscover the old. (Consider, for example, the Rosetta Stone that unlocked the writing of our ancestors.)

Community documentation projects help us identify information that is missing from the historical record. Once we determine what aspects of society are not being recorded, including our intangible heritage, we can devise ways to capture information about them. Oral history projects, recipe gatherings, craft exhibits, and other concerted efforts to bring together those with specific knowledge so that they may transfer it to someone who can document it are valuable for accurately continuing our community memories.

Considering a history beyond your own provides an opportunity to be even more creative with your information capturing. Oral history, collaborative scrapbooks, and neighborhood histories all have the potential for documenting neglected information in a really unique way.[53] What "intangible heritage" do your communities treasure? How do you contribute to it, and how can you help save it?

---

[53] Linda Norris, "How Do You Put People in the Picture of Local History? 2 Smart Ideas," *The Uncataloged Museum*, November 2010, uncatalogedmuseum.blogspot.com/2010/11/how-do-you-put-people-in-picture-of.html (July 27, 2011). See Linda's blogs at www.blogger.com/profile/02833927749919826650.

Mental and Writing Exercises for Unrecorded History

1. Based on your earlier work with organization (and description if you chose to do it), reexamine and list what important aspects of your life you have already acknowledged to be undocumented.

2. Think about your family stories and traditions. Review objects in your home. Mull over your "quirky habits." Now, if appropriate, add more things to your list of important aspects of your life that should be documented that you previously did not consider.

3. Write a bulleted list describing the events of a "typical" day in your household. Examine this list and think about which of these things have corresponding documentation. Are there any activities that shed light on your lifestyle and personality that are not being documented in some way?

4. Put an asterisk next to three undocumented things on your bulleted list. Consider various ways you can record information about them.

5. Focus on a single event or favorite activity. Write a recent memory of your participation in that activity. You can write in paragraphs or bulleted lists, or you can create a mind map. Alternately, record yourself talking about the event. How would you expand the project to include the points of view of others who participated in the activities? What other forms of documentation could you include?

6. Think about your "sense of place." What role does your place play in your life story? List five things that make your place unique and describe how these unique elements have impacted you.

7. List five forms of intangible heritage that are important to your life. How can you record information about them?

Chapter Seven:
Electronic Information

Experiencing Archives: My 3.5-Inch Floppies

I have a small box of treasured disks in my closet. They contain the information that started my career—the volumes I wrote in grad school about how great the archives world is and the materials I devised to help my first library start up its archives department. All of my early brilliance sits on these gorgeously colored, and virtually unreadable, backups.

I do have to add that I have an archives box that holds printed versions of my most wonderful creations. (Hurray for the old-fashioned me!) But I do wonder what is on those disks. I'm sure there is a bit of forgotten brilliance somewhere.

Do you think your DVDs will be readable forever? Think again. If you have not already, keep abreast of innovation and migrate your information as necessary.

The Digital World

I do not need to tell you that the world is changing. The way we create and keep information is very different now from the way it was ten years ago. It is beyond the scope of this book to explain standards in digital archives management, but I would like to give you a glimpse at where we are heading and what you can do to make sure that the digital information you have created is preserved for posterity. This book, up until this point, has discussed electronic information only peripherally. This chapter focuses on the whole of our digital documentation, its context, and ways to manage the resources.

Although our production of paper records as a society has not dropped, we are moving more and more of our everyday functions to a digital realm. We are caught between two worlds. The information that we kept on paper calendars, in written correspondence, on recipe cards, and the like is slowly moving to our computer. Be aware of the crossover and think about the viability of the information you now see on your laptop or smart phone as opposed to the information you once kept on tangible paper.

We are in transition, and some say that we are entering a sort of Dark Age, where it will be hard to access the information we create today in tomorrow's world. If we do not think about how we are creating our information and how we plan to see it in the future, we are effectively relinquishing much of the knowledge we are generating to a black hole.

We can easily see evidence of this technical innovation problem in information we created a century ago. Many films from the early twentieth century have been destroyed by time. We did not effectively preserve them and so they are gone. This is the same for audio recordings.

The media itself is degrading, and we are also losing the tools that allow us to see information. Technology is changing so fast that we sometimes throw aside the old and bring in the new without thinking. For instance, when we return to view the old images from our 1970s filmstrips, we find the projectors hard to come by. Archivists and museums are scrambling to keep the tools that will allow us to read the information that we have created. It may be too late for some; in other cases, the machines are so few that it is difficult to locate one that we are allowed to use. This is especially true for home recordings if we are not professionals in the business.

The problems we have with audio and video are magnified by digital. For one thing, many past formats were visible without equipment, if not ideally viewed this way. Old filmstrips and film cameras

Backup, Backup, Backup!

Digital materials can disappear quite quickly and unexpectedly. One day you are looking at a document on your computer, and the next day you cannot get to it. Like paper documents, personal digital files are lost every day. Unlike paper files, that loss can happen in the blink of an eye. The best way to avoid digital loss is to back up your information. We do not know how long data will last on certain media. CDs, for example, have highly varying lifespans depending on their manufacturing. Their longevity can even vary from one batch to another in the same brand. To be safest, keep backups in diverse formats and places. Consider backing up the files on your computer onto a separate hard drive in your home for easy access. Explore options for off-site storage through a company that specializes in this. You might even consider something as simple as keeping a hard drive at a friend's house. A good rule of thumb is to keep three copies, backing up to one separate space regularly. If possible, schedule automatic backups to a home server.

Digital Preservation Standard

In order to ensure that our digital information can be read in the future, it is advantageous to save the information using a standard format. Differing formats have advantages and disadvantages for long term use. Proprietary programs such as Microsoft Word and Photoshop have no guarantees for their survival. In fact, I have many old Word Processing files that I can no longer read. According to the Association for Information and Image Management (AIIM), TIFF and XML are widely adopted formats that have good and bad aspects to them. They, and other standards like them, do not capture all the information in a file necessary to understand its structure, appearance, tagging systems, and content. Though PDF cannot guarantee information preservation, it currently comes closest to ensuring the long term viability of your information. PDF/A has been adopted as an ISO standard that is mandated and reliable. Furthermore, research into its viability is ongoing. Whenever possible, use this format to save your documents.

left negatives that we could see by holding them up to a light source. We are moving further and further away from this simplicity. We thought that the audiotapes we could not hear without a recorder were a preservation nightmare. Now we are even creating digital files that cannot be seen without a decryption key that gives us access to the information.[54] This raises questions such as: How can we successfully pass that key on to the people who have a legitimate right to it in the future?

Think of all the formats we have for different things— JPEGs, .txt files, PDFs, etc. Do you know what formats are best for retaining items so you have a good chance of seeing them in the future?[55] Furthermore, what about the transient nature of digital information? Are you texting? Is there any information in the text that you might want to retain in some kind of permanent form? What about your Skype sessions? And finally, to whom do you trust the care of your information? Is your whole life history on

---

[54] A decryption key is used to translate an encoded message. We encrypt (or cipher) information to protect privacy.
[55] "Image File Format Standards: TIFF, JPEG, and PDF. Different Formats for Different Jobs," *AIIM*, January/February 2006, www.aiim.org/Infonomics/ArticleView.aspx?id=31178 (July 29, 2011).

Facebook? What will Facebook do with the information, and will the social networking site even be around in 30 years? Where would the information go if Facebook disappeared? What about other sites you use—the places you put pictures, or keep your blog, or upload your business contacts?

There is no guarantee that any of these places will survive into the future. No matter what the drawbacks to the personal papers and digital archives in your home, you are the one with the control. You do not have full control when you put information online and trust it to another.

Then there is the question of organization. Do you keep your items neatly arranged in folders on your own desktop? How do you keep track of what you have out in cyberspace? If you were hit by a bus tomorrow, would your family even know where to look for your information?[56] It is no longer centralized in an easily accessible shoebox, the trunk of your car, or a safe deposit box at the local bank.

From the previous questions, it is clear that many of the issues we have with digital files are similar to the problems we have with our paper documents, but things get more complicated in the digital ream. Just like paper, we can lose track of documents, and they degrade. However, because of the ease with which we create and distribute information and the need for

If I Disappeared Tomorrow, Would You Remember Me?

When someone dies, what happens to their digital information? Well, unless you make specialized plans for your data, it stays right where it is. What do you want people to remember about you? Unmanaged, your private information might be seen down the road by those who you do not wish to access it. Your kids may find information about your wild partying. Or, more seriously, your former identity could be stolen, causing serious problems for your loved ones who are left behind. Companies such as Entrustet, Legacy Locker, and My Webwill help you leave your "digital assets" to a person you designate, allowing them to manage or close down your online personal accounts. Consider what aspects of your digital self you should pass on and what should just fade away with time.

---

[56] Erica Swallow, "7 Ways to Handle Digital Life After Death," *Mashable*, mashable.com/2010/10/11/social-media-after-death (July 29, 2011).

an intermediary tool to view it, we have created a wide range of other problems that we need to address. Unfortunately, all too frequently, we take the existence of our digital information for granted and are even less likely to address needs for appraisal, organization, preservation, and access than we are for printed files. We assume the files will be there when we need them and the computer will do the work of "archivist."

In reality, the inability to see our information directly and the far-flung existence of some of our information on computers outside of our own personal space can make its preservation and the likelihood of its longevity even less secure. Barring disaster, a box of files sitting in my closet will always be there for me to peek at, even if its form has some degradation. A file that I placed on the Internet can disappear in a nanosecond. Even more alarming, a file sitting on a computer in my home is equally at risk. It can be destroyed in a proverbial puff of smoke with a not-rare-enough computer crash or with disk damage.[57] The disasters we concerned ourselves with our papers do not need to take a catastrophic form in the digital world—it can occur simply by clicking and dragging an item to the wrong place.

On the plus side, the ease with which we create information today means that there is more documentation about our lives that is being recorded. The possibility that this information can exist for future generations is exciting. If we preserve our memories properly, humanity will have greater knowledge of our lives and our communities, with the possibility of a better understanding of our interconnectedness. So much insight into the way people work, play, and think can help propel us toward a greater future civilization where ideas help promote innovation and collaboration.

---

[57] Sometimes, the information we think we have lost because of a computer malfunction or digital degradation can be recovered by a computer specialist. Consider this option for important personal digital files that you cannot recover on your own.

Personal Computer

Let us start by considering the maintenance of something on the easier side. Consider the management of the contained files that sit on your personal computer. These are the files to which you alone have access. You write documents and keep them ordered within folders. Like an old-fashioned file cabinet, this means of structuring our records requires us to choose logical topics for the ordered maintenance of our materials.

Luckily, on the computer, the search function serves as a sort of finding aid that allows us to locate material that has been misfiled or that proves elusive when our common sense about where we would put something today does not match the common sense we used yesterday to place it. As long as we can remember what is in the file, a portion of the name, or the date that we created it, we should be able to retrieve it easily.

The system can break down in a number of ways:

- We can totally forget about a file and it just hangs out there until we stumble upon it one day.
- We keep multiple versions of a file and forget which one is the master.
- The file disappears because we misnamed it or put it in the wrong folder, and the "Search" command is not helping because you cannot

What Do You Consider Your "Personal Computer?"

My PC used to be my desktop. Then, my laptop became my main computer. Now people can carry around a multitude of devices with personal computer-type functions. Your smart phone, your e-book reader, and your iPad are all devices on which you leave bits of your life and your personal documentation. The organization and preservation of the information on all of these devices needs to be managed to ensure the security of your files. Organize your resources as logically on each as you do on your "traditional" personal computer. Plug in and back up your information regularly. Await the next generation of electronic devices that will encourage the migration of your data. Changing from one system to another gets easier all the time, but do not be complacent and take it for granted. Be prepared by securing your information and keeping track of it.

remember appropriate keywords to search.

Figure 37. My current file structure for organizing my active work on my personal computer.

As with your print files, think big. What large record groups and series can logically hold your files in a neat way? Consider the flow you will seek when it comes time for you to browse your files to find what you need. As a librarian, I once regularly taught introductory computer classes and now do so sporadically as a consultant. For the past twenty years, I have told people to think of the documents on their computer as documents in a filing cabinet. This seems to be the most useful explanation so that non–computer users or non-organizer-type people can understand the concept of organizing digital files. Order your folders in the same way you would order the drawers and the files of your cabinet—with logical headings and a manageable number of folders. Do not make multiple copies of your materials on the same machine. Always file (i.e., place a document in the proper folder) when you create it.

Both Windows and Apple computers set you up for success in this area should you choose to adopt their plan. Use their "My Documents" folder and place your own subheadings within it. I have seen people create confusion out of their folder structure by placing materials within folders for the type of software they use to create the document, rather than within logical subject areas they create. Do not place all your Word files with the Word program. Do not place all your pictures with your Canon software. I have also seen people get confused with too many folders. Every file — or two, or three — does not need its own folder.

For example, you can place all of your weekend getaway images in one folder. Will you really remember if you happily ran into an old friend while on vacation and took your picture with her before or after breakfast? Will you be able to seek the proper folder from the right hour of the day to find her? Or, will you be just as happy to browse through your fifty images of the day all neatly kept together to find the picture you took to remind you of the moment? You do not necessarily need a folder for every activity. Your images of your hotel, walk through the park, and visit to the museum can all be placed together. Order your images so it is not a hassle to move from folder to folder.

Although backing up your images is important, making

Born Digital

In 2010, Emory University acquired the personal papers of Salman Rushdie. Of particular note in the collection is digital material from four of Rushdie's computers and a hard drive. Archivists made the decision to try to emulate the experience of looking through Rushdie's computers for this series in the collection, rather than providing a "traditional" archives experience. Processing digital materials is a challenge to archivists. The Rushdie archives is the first to seek a method for coordinating this kind of archives project. Few repositories are collecting "born digital" information, and when they do, they concentrate on preservation and storage. As with printed folders, the original order of materials can be revealing. The choices we make when creating documents—our edits, our organizational structures, the software applications we choose to use, and more—provide important information about us and our activities. If we can save the clues to those thought processes, we should. Finding ways to capture an individual's digital documentation and its context in full is a great and exciting challenge to my profession.

multiple copies of one file on one computer is detrimental to your sanity. When librarian colleagues once transferred their paper files to the archives in which I worked for safekeeping, I was perplexed by how often I received multiple paper copies of one article or flyer. These duplicates were exactly the same and not drafts that showed a progression in thought. Sometimes there were copies of the same document among many folders. I am still not sure if this is a preservation technique, a way to easily access materials for handouts when needed, or a complicated organizational method. The rule of thumb is, whether on the computer or in print: Keep one master copy, and keep well-planned backups. Do not randomly sprinkle materials throughout a collection with the hope that you can easily stumble across a copy when you need it. Too many copies confuse the chronology of their creation. How often do you lose track of which copy is your master and which are old drafts? When I am not careful, this happens to me quite easily, especially when I start keeping duplicates of files across multiple folder structures. Instead, I aim to keep materials in one place. If materials are digital, I keep backups on other computers and in other mediums. Keep a folder titled "Old Drafts" if you think that you need them for reference. Keep the drafts folder in your "archives" (think long-term documents that you will not manipulate) to show your progression of thought.

Oftentimes, computer users keep files that were started and never finished or that are no longer used on a regular basis. Amass your computer files as you would your paper files. Institute a records management plan that allows you to discard what is unnecessary by trashing it or moving it to alternate "archival" storage. For example, I have marketing materials that I created for my business when I started it ten years ago. My logo has changed. I no longer use the same program to design similar materials, and my whole business philosophy has grown so that these materials no longer properly represent my work. There is no reason to keep these files on my main computer in my active "Marketing" folder. I have ensured that they are in my backup storage spots in the "archives."

Personal Communication

Most of us now correspond through e-mail, Twitter, Facebook, and texting. However, the sending of bits and bytes has only been our prime form of written communication for about ten years. People still retain old written letters from friends and family, personal notes and greetings, and formal correspondence in file boxes and cabinets. Written expression has been a major form of communication since the beginning of civilized society. We first exchanged ideas in writing on rocks and cave walls and later moved to papyrus and other more portable forms that allowed us to become more prolific writers. Digital resources have made it even easier to jot down our thoughts, continuing the evolutionary process of our writing. We must view all the various written ways we communicate as a whole, saving what is most important for ourselves and posterity.[58]

It is interesting to note that in addition to the format change, the evolution of correspondence has changed what we say and how we say it. For one, modern correspondence tools allow us to give information to many people at once rather than sending one message at a time. We can do this to specific people with e-mail, but we can also spread a message to strangers via social networking sites. Things that were once private are now becoming public. Additionally, as we share more and more, we

The Battle to Save Letters

Some people bemoan the loss of the old-fashioned handwritten letter. There is something about opening a box of old papers with your mother's handwriting on her favorite stationery to make you feel like she is right next to you, whispering in your ear. Though I adore the old letter, I am a great admirer of modern correspondence, too. Though Mom lives across the country, I can easily catch her online each evening for a quick written chat. My challenge is to preserve this marvelous digital documentation she gives me. In my case, when my daughter leaves home, she will be grateful to correspond with me via computer. I have awful handwriting!

---

[58] Most of this section was originally published in "Lost Letters" on the ArchivesInfo blog on October 28, 2010.

write fewer and fewer words in one shot to do it. Because social networks and e-mail are virtually free and we can make use of them with tools that are available to us at any time, we are tending to write in shorter bursts and more often than in the past. It is now uncommon for one to sit and write an in-depth description of one's week to mail off to a far-off loved one. Many would rather just write something such as "Baby took first steps this morn" on our Facebook walls and let a back-and-forth dialogue ensue.

As technology makes the communication itself easier, in many ways it makes the saving of collections of correspondence related to our lives more difficult. On the positive side, e-mail has made it easier for us to save copies of our correspondence. In the past, one had to make a concerted effort to make carbon copies of our letters or to photocopy them before sending if we wanted to retain back and forth communiqués. Today, our computer systems keep both sides of correspondence within our software programs, so we can easily see what someone has written to us alongside our reply. But how do we separate the important e-mails from the dull ones—and what about those text messages, blog posts, and tweets? The Library of Congress has announced a program to "archive" Tweets, but we do not yet know how ancestors may be able to access them in the future.

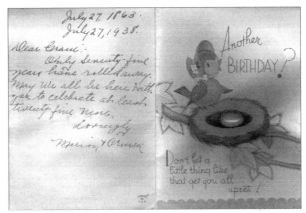

Figure 38. Despite e-cards and other creative ways to send greetings online, the stationery card industry has made a comeback and is growing despite the recession in 2010, according to Research and Markets reports. This card from the 1930s is typical of the period:[59] "Dear Gram: Only seventy-five years have rolled away. May we all be here with you to celebrate at least twenty-five more. Lovingly, Marion and Orman."

---

[59] "Greeting Cards and eCards in the United States 2010," Research and Markets, February 2010, www.researchandmarkets.com/reports/1207465/greeting_cards_and_ecards_in_the_united_states (July 29, 2011).

How many people think about how family might be able to treasure your e-mails and other digitized words? It is advantageous for those of us thinking about the value of our correspondence to use programs that back up Twitter and Facebook accounts. Keep your important and interesting e-mails organized in folders, and think of these folders as you would the old-fashioned kind. Label them so the files inside make sense and are easily accessible. Also, be aware that digital files can be lost in the blink of an eye. Make at least two well-managed copies of everything that are logically organized in folders where you can find them. Keep the copies in alternate formats and retain one off-site. Be prepared to migrate the data as technology keeps changing. For small home collections, it is always acceptable, from a home archives preservation perspective, to print what is most important to you and save it the old-fashioned way, in preservation-safe folders, just to be sure.

We are in the midst of a great change in communication. For now, we must still keep an eye toward the old way of doing things while automation changes rapidly. The crossover to a digital world is only just beginning. The implications of lost correspondence are troubling for both the purpose of scholarship and family/community memory.

Figure 39. Christmas greetings are still primarily delivered by the United States Postal Service in this country, though the letters that once accompanied cards seem to be dwindling.

Creating a Sense of Place Digitally

According to the SepiaTown website, SepiaTown "lets you view and share thousands of mapped historical images from around the globe." It is a participatory project that encourages visitors to help document a community in a digital environment. Images spread across the world come together on this centralized site to help tell a story that was previously scattered. This visual representation of a global society is a project that helps alleviate problems associated with unwritten history, creating collections of multiple "donations" of photos that provide a sense of place in a way that each image on its own cannot.

www.sepiatown.com

Photographs

I think the most obvious example of how changing technology has affected our personal archives in the past ten years is the way we handle photographs. My daughter looks at my old negatives in awe. A negative is a magical thing to her. She better understands the small card that holds my digital files in my camera until I move them to my computer. She can hardly fathom a time when you could not see the image in a screen on the back of a picture-taking device and when you could not take a picture with a phone. She is accustomed to watching me save files in folders on my computer, pick the best ones to upload onto the Internet for Grandma and Grandpa to see in Florida, and then save everything to a backup drive before deleting from the camera card. I continually use, change, and distribute these images. I add them to websites. I print some out on my special photo printer. I encourage family members to order copies online. I make family calendars. I use some images on blogs and social media sites. I change colors and sizes. All of these things were unimaginable just a short time ago.

Images are ubiquitous. They once had a sense of specialness. In the nineteenth century, people dressed for them. It was out of the ordinary to make an appointment with a photographer. In fact, it may have only occurred once in a lifetime. In the twentieth century, we could take our own photographs, but we still had to plan. We had to remember to bring the camera. We had to make a special trip to get pictures developed or mail them out. Today, people regularly carry around photo-taking devices and incorporate them into their daily lives. If I see a new sink I like while browsing through my local big-box hardware store, I can snap a photo, text it to my husband, and ask him if he thinks I should buy it for our bathroom remodel. There is certainly nothing special about that image.

It is easy to lose track of what pictures should be valued for posterity among the thousands we take each year. The ease with which we create images these days and the low price—virtually free after you purchase your camera, with only the cost of a re-chargeable battery and extra memory cards—means that we have a proliferation of images that run easily out of control. You should appropriately label and organize photos so that you can easily find them when you want them. Photo-organizing software encourages you to add keywords or descriptors that will make them easy to find. Use the same principles to organize photos as you would organize documents on your computer.

Additionally, similar to

Flickr Commons

Flickr is used by individuals for their personal photo collections and also by large professional repositories. According to their website, "The key goals of The Commons on Flickr are to firstly show you hidden treasures in the world's public photography archives, and secondly to show how your input and knowledge can help make these collections even richer." Flickr invites online users to leave comments about images or to add "tags" (keywords or descriptors) that are easily searchable and that allow searchers to more easily find items related to specific people, places, and events. Some of the largest photo collections in the world are represented here, including images from places such as the National Archives in the U.S. and the U.K., the Reykjavik Museum, and the Swedish National Heritage Board. The site is a way to make images from repositories more accessible and to apply "crowdsourcing" techniques, which seek user input to expand knowledge and explore subjects in diverse ways.

www.flickr.com/commons

Photo Management

I like the ACDSee Photo Manager for organizing my personal files. There are many packages on the market that do the same thing. Some such as PaintShop Photo Pro and Adobe Photoshop incorporate photo management into photo-editing capabilities. The software allows you to point to images in folders across your computer. (You should have arranged most of them safely by date in a photo folder.) You can then add tags to images to make them easy to find later. At the very least, include the event and subject name. The camera software should include the date the image was taken. Add other pertinent information. Keep your tags as consistent as possible, standardizing your information. Make sure the words you choose are plural or singular and do not change. Settle on names for certain subjects and stick with them. For example, do not call photos of your place of dwelling "home" in some pictures and "house" in others because this will make it more difficult to find what you need. The software will help you identify words you have used in the past. Try to be as detailed as possible, thinking ahead to others who may try to access these photos. Instead of photos of "Mom," use your mother's full name and consider defining your relationship within the photo managing software or in a separate guide to your imagery.

correspondence, today we maintain photographs locally and on the Internet. It is very easy to lose track of the original image. A master photo should be preserved on your computer, in-house server, or separate backup hard drive. One of my personal control issues with my own files is that I find the time to label only some of my images. When I am not careful, before I know it, I have lost track of the original file, forgotten who the people are in the photograph, or allowed the digital information to degrade so much that I can never open that file again. The challenge that we all must address is finding the time to properly manage our materials and establish a workflow that makes it less of a chore.

It is a good idea to use a photo software database package to organize your files with thumbnails that point to the originals and allow you to "tag" pictures by adding keywords that pertain to the images. These keywords enable you to search for the files you need when you need them. You do not have to continually rearrange photos into folders that make sense: You can simply download them from your camera, organize them by date, and let your software do the heavy work. As with all things in the digital world, keep backups of both your original photo files and your software data that links to it.

Maintaining photos online is useful for sharing and browsing your images. Many people use online photo-share sites such as Kodak™, iPrintfromHome™, Shutterfly™, Flickr™, Photobucket™, and SmugMug™ as backup storage and for keeping easily sharable albums. There are two caveats if you wish to do this. They both relate to the fact that you are putting your materials onto a site owned by someone else. For one, the site could disappear tomorrow and you could lose your backup method. For another, your images might not be as private as you think they are. Consider what you put online and if it is appropriate to share.

Formats for Saving Digital Photos

JPEG—Though most of us save our pictures this way, this format does not save all of one's image information. The advantage is that JPEG results in a small image size that is easy to manage and can be easily read by a wide variety of software programs. Information is compressed to make a small file size. Simply put, images can become a bit blurrier and colors can be inexact.

TIF (a.k.a. TIFF)—TIFF is widely recognized as the format of choice for archiving important images. It is supported across diverse software formats and does not compress in the same way that JPEG does. It is considered the standard for keeping your photos for the long term, but a file takes up more space than a JPEG: When you have a choice for saving your important images, choose this one (for example, your wedding photo that you may enlarge to 20x30 one day).

RAW—You may have heard about RAW, so I want to briefly include it here. RAW includes all your information without any in-the-camera software interpretation. In other words, you need to do a lot of work to take a great picture and to convert it to the image you are accustomed to seeing. RAW files are also very large, so unless you are a professional photographer or serious hobbyist, you will not be using this format.

AIIM. "Image File Format Standards: TIFF, JPEG, and PDF. Different Formats for Different Jobs." January/February 2006. www.aiim.org/Infonomics/ArticleView.aspx?id=31178 (July 31, 2011)

Community Facebook Page

Seeking to "reconstitute" the community in which I grew up, I created a private Facebook page specifically for my former neighbors. Other Facebook users ask to be made members of the group. If I remember someone from my childhood or someone else in the group can vouch for them as a former resident of our neighborhood community, I grant them membership. On this page, we reminisce about life on our street. We catch up on what is happening to our members and post photos of ourselves. Our community Facebook page has been a great way to reconnect with people I once viewed as a second family, allowing me to preserve a community that I thought I had lost long ago and connecting my past and my present in ways I couldn't have imagined twenty years ago.

Re-creating "Real" Life Online

When I write "re-creating your real life online," I am not referring to creating an avatar (caricature of yourself) to explore computer-simulated living spaces. There are so many things that we do (or did) away from the computer that we now accomplish in a virtual reality. From socializing with our friends to shopping for Christmas presents, the things we do online can substitute or enhance our real-life relationships and activities. As we grow more and more dependent on computer interaction, we leave larger fragments of our personal documentation on the Internet. When we are truthful and are not trying to create an online alter ego, this information reveals a lot about who we are as people, just as "traditional" printed information does. By evaluating our online interactions, one can often create a good picture of what a person is like, how that person functions in society, and how society is affected by that person's actions.

Our online documentation is often valuable for our personal archives. We need to consider how we are projecting ourselves and how our online selves are a re-creation of our offline selves. How does the online documentation dovetail with the offline personal papers that we learned to appraise and maintain in earlier chapters? How can we similarly deal with the new material?

Much of what I do online is not very revealing from an historical perspective. For example, I will go out on a limb to say that the office supplies I sporadically purchase online and have delivered to my home do not rank among the vital data that I need to save. It is useful instead to compare my unique interactions with the online world with my real life—the correspondence I write and receive, the stories I write and share, and the special sites to which I provide content using my opinions and knowledge.

Today, we have the opportunity to save everything if we have the time, forethought, and organizational aptitude to do it.[60] Computer space is relatively cheap. However, just like our noncomputerized documentation, it is more realistic to cull the highlights of our online lives to present them to future generations. Keeping track of what is important to us and most revealing about us will allow us to continue to pass on the material that will matter most to our families and to future generations. Much of what I put online is a bit serendipitous. On my personal social media sites, for example, I post what strikes me at the moment. This seems to mimic most of my real-life interactions. However, the strange thing about interacting with the world this way is that it is really not like real life. I may "say" things online that I really would not say in person or that would never get documented in person. How do I determine what is worth saving? This is a great challenge for the future.

"I Love Making Content"

A fellow blogger recently told me, "I love making content!" Contributing to social media sites and creating your own Web pages allows an individual to explore areas of interest and to share their passions with others. We now have an opportunity to make our voices heard by being active participants in an online world and by contributing to historical documentation in a way we could not before the Internet. You have the power to make some of the materials that researchers will use in the future to better understand our society. Feel free to use it to make content that expresses your personality and world view.

---

[60] "Lifestreaming" is an attempt to track all of the streams of information flowing through our electronic systems. Unlike archives management, this form of managing information advocates for saving everything. Read more about it on the Lifestream homepage by Eric Freeman and David Gelernter (cs-www.cs.yale.edu/homes/freeman/lifestreams.html).

Mental and Writing Exercises for Electronic Information

1. Do you have any digital records in your home that you can no longer access? Consider if any of these files have valuable information that you should have a computer specialist attempt to recover for you.

2. Take a look at the files on your computer. Have you created organized folders that are appropriate for holding logical groupings of records? How can your system be improved? Does your file structure adequately reflect how you work and what is important to you?

3. Make a list of all the sites where you post information online. Should any of this information be backed up to another location for its safekeeping? Is this information an accurate reflection of your life? Does it supplement other recorded documentation you keep on your home computer or in printed form?

4. Review your personal correspondence in paper and digital formats. How can you link the files in some kind of finding aid? For example, can you make a series note called "correspondence" that describes your paper letters and your e-mails?

5. Consider how your tweets, Facebook statuses, and other social media amend your correspondence and other files. Do they offer an interesting additional dimension to your life story? If so, make sure you back up the files.

6. Review your digital photographs and consider their maintenance. Are your images appropriately organized and labeled? Do you have at least two local copies? Have you considered your online privacy and security?

7. Have you created computerized "archives" consisting of organized folders and documents that you are no longer actively manipulating? Make sure your active digital files and your "archives" are separated, just as with your paper files.

Chapter Eight:
Planning for the Future

Your Family and Your Archives

- Preserve the context of your materials. Describe your collection to the best of your abilities.
- Preserve and organize your materials so that the person(s) who will care for them in the future has little work to do to maintain them.
- Fill gaps in your stories with personal documentation projects.
- Reach out and share your stories with loved ones during your lifetime. Use your archives as a launching point for discussions.
- Treat your archives as you treat other beloved family heirlooms by regarding them as a valuable resource and worthwhile inheritance.

Passing Personal Papers to Loved Ones

One prime value of your personal papers relates to their usefulness during your lifetime. They help you remember your past, evaluate your life, and organize your activities. A second value of your materials relates to the use of your records when you no longer need them, and then after you are gone. One should formally prepare for the transfer of one's archives to a designated person who will care for them as precious historical information.[61]

First, consider members of your family who take an interest in your history. If possible, designate a relative to whom you will give your personal papers. Be sure to incorporate a discussion of the placement of your personal archives in your last will and testament if you do not plan to pass your materials on before your death. If you have created a finding aid for your materials, include it with your will so that it is clear what your personal archives collection encompasses. During your lifetime, discuss your plans and desires to pass your materials on with the person who you would like to receive them. Consider recording your conversation to include with your collection. Give your designated person a copy of the finding aid.

---

[61] Throughout this book, I have tried to impress the meaning of archives as information with long-term value beyond their useful life. Plans for the future of your personal papers should pay particular attention, once again, to materials that have value for posterity.

Throughout your lifetime, be sure to explain the value of your personal family history to loved ones. Incorporate traditions into your lives and discuss your heritage. Teach children why they should value these things. I often hear people at my presentations discussing how their children are not interested in their family history or their "old stuff." One must help children build an appreciation for the past. It may be harder to hold on to past values in a fast-paced digital world, but it is not impossible. With the knowledge you have gained from this book and the innate desire you have to preserve your past, you can teach children the value of records and historical memory.[62]

Value of Personal Papers for Archives Repositories

There are times when there is no one within your family to whom you can give your collection of personal papers. There are also times when the community value of your collection outweighs its family value. Or, you and your family members may decide that your collection will be better maintained or put to better use within a formal institution. Many archives repositories seek personal papers for their collections. The personal papers that you keep in your home may provide valuable perceptions about a particular time and lifestyle. It may clarify our understanding about historical happenings or provide useful information about how society changes over time. Early in this book, we discussed the value of archives to communities beyond those you recognize as your own. This chapter discusses how to reach out

Repositories That May Take Interest in Your Personal Papers

Consider the institutions that will make best use of your materials and the collections that are the best fit for your personal story.

- Local and state historical societies
- Academic Archives with specialized interests
- Genealogical libraries/Archives
- Professional and association Archives
- Libraries/Archives /museums with specialized information or interests

---

[62] For more on teaching the value of history to children, see "Don't Know (Or Care) Much about History," *ArchivesInfo* blog, October 2010, archivesinfo.blogspot.com/2010/10/dont-know-or-care-much-about-history.html (July 27, 2011).

Considerations to Identify the Proper Repository for Your Materials

Did all of the people represented in your family collection come from the same locale, and do the records reflect a sense of place?

Do your papers reflect the lifestyle of people living in a particular time or people of a specific ethnic background?

Did any of the people reflected in your collection do anything especially noteworthy?

Are any well-known historic events described in your materials?

Did any of the people in your collection immigrate or migrate?

Are your materials written in another language?

Are there any particular subjects of interest or hobbies represented among your items?

and find people who are interested in your archival material, and it will explain how to share your information with them.

By now, you know that personal papers tell the stories of individual lives and provide valuable information about the diverse ways in which we live. Repositories treasure personal views about various eras. The records families create are the primary sources that often provide the best insight into activities, revealing previously unknown information about historical events that seemed set in stone by the "official" accounts we have retained in institutions. History is a pliable thing. Our knowledge about the past grows as we uncover more collections over time and attach new insight and understanding to time-honored recollections of events.

Professional archives repositories retain policies that describe their holdings, the strengths of their resources, and the types of materials they are seeking to expand their collections. Repositories are looking to develop relationships with researchers interested in these sources, but they also should be looking to identify people who harbor information that is important to the history they are trying to preserve, protect, and interpret. Generally, repositories seek archives that fall within their collection development policy's guidelines. They may be offered records by citizens, but it is also useful for them to actively work to identify citizens who retain materials related to the particular subjects that interest them. Archives want a better understanding of what documentation has been created and what survives to better understand the extent of the historical record.

It is helpful to create a relationship with an organization to which you may donate your records in the future. This helps the repository better understand what documentation materials are available in their collecting area of interest. This may aid them to better serve researchers. This will also enable them to provide you with information about the proper maintenance of materials, so you can give them appropriate attention for their security as soon as possible. Forming a relationship with a collecting organization familiarizes you with their methods and policies so you can more easily donate if you wish to do so in the future.

Develop a mindset that considers your records beyond their active lives, making them more important as documents of social activity and not just papers to be used and disposed or hidden away. Take notice of your recordkeeping behavior and see your materials as valuable assets of cultural heritage.

Explaining Your Family

This photograph from my parents' wedding features my grandparents. To the left is my step-grandfather. His wife, my father's mother, is in the middle. My mother's father is to the right. If I were to give my papers to a repository, an explanation of what happened to my father's natural dad and my mother's mom would be helpful to understand this image in context. The information associated with the image explains not only what we are seeing in this picture, but can also include quite a bit about my parents, my relationships with them, and my own view of my family. Furthermore, this image reflects a particular time, place, and larger social community.

Splitting Papers

The writer and mistress of H. G. Wells, Rebecca West, donated her papers to the Beinecke library in 1955, but this collection "is far from complete. Papers left at her death were sold by West's estate to the University of Tulsa in Oklahoma. Numerous letters are still in private hands. A major collection was [recently] sold." With all good intentions to secure her legacy, West did not successfully cement the future of her letters. The primary documents related to this remarkable woman's life are spread across collections. Many have also been destroyed.

Be clear about where you want your documentation to go and take appropriate steps.

Finding the Right Repository for Your Family Papers

If you are looking to donate your family papers or if you are seeking to contact an organization that retains information related to the materials in your possession, there are a number of things for you to consider.[63] The most suitable place for your materials may be local, or it could be across the country. In certain cases, your materials may be appropriate for a foreign repository. In the digital age, it is much easier for you to find a proper home for your items than it was just a decade ago. Consider all of the subjects represented in your materials that may interest a researcher—occupations, religion, hobbies, locale, etc.—and seek repositories that accommodate that focus in their collections.

In some cases, your family papers may be a perfect fit for more than one repository. My rule of thumb is to try to keep items local if possible. Additionally, you should usually try to keep your materials together as one collection.[64] If someone comes searching for information about your family, they will likely want

---

[63] See "A Guide to Donating Your Personal or Family Papers to a Repository," *The Society of American Archivists,* www.archivists.org/publications/donating-familyrecs.asp (July 29, 2011).
[64] For more information about Rebecca West's collections described in the text box, read an excerpt of *Selected Letters of Rebecca West* in *The New York Times Book Review* (http://www.nytimes.com/books/first/w/west-letters.html).
"Rebecca West Papers," *Department of Special Collections and University Archive. University of Tulsa,* www.lib.utulsa.edu/speccoll/collections/westrebecca/index.htm (July 29, 2011).
"Rebecca West Collection," *Beinecke Rare Book and Manuscript Library, Yale University,* hdl.handle.net/10079/fa/beinecke.westart (July 29, 2011).

information about multiple generations. In rare cases, it might be appropriate to split collections. For example, if your father was a famous scientist and your mother was a famous author, her papers may go to a repository that specializes in writers, and his may go to a science research center. In general, though, if your materials do not reflect multiple uncommon lives, family papers should stay together.

It is advantageous to keep materials together in one logical place so that a researcher does not have to travel or search extensively. Additionally, keeping materials together allows one to see a collection as a whole, intact, as it existed in your possession. This adheres to the principle of "provenance" described earlier in the book. Though digitization has made it easier for us to link collections across institutions in collaborative projects, it is still a good idea to keep the originals together for researcher edification and to preserve the authentic nature of the collection. There will be times when someone wants or needs to see the originals and not just digitized copies of paper records. Your materials as a collection provide much insight into your life, your communities, and the culture around you. Splitting your collection weakens its informational value. The many intellectual connections one might make about your life and a deeper understanding of your role in the world can be lost when materials are

Providing Context for Your Materials

The following is a list of some basic information that would be useful to the repository receiving your collection:

- Biography basics—birth dates, death dates, marriages, residences, occupations
- List family members and describe relationships (even include a family tree if you can)
- List previous owners of the collection with dates
- Note any outstanding life events—schooling, important trips, awards
- Date documents if possible
- If the significance of certain materials is not obvious, clarify it
- If the materials do not relate directly to your family, describe how you acquired them, from whom, when, and why

Questions to Ask a Repository

What is your storage area like? Will the materials I am proposing to donate be kept in a climate-controlled space? If you do not have climate control, have your storage areas been tested for fluctuations in temperature and humidity? What is your shelving like? Is it preservation safe? Are materials raised at least four to six inches off the floor on the lowest shelf?

Do you use preservation-safe materials for the storage of your collections?

What kind of backlog does the institution have? When can I expect you to make my materials accessible to researchers? When will a finding aid be complete? Does the institution make unprocessed collections available to researchers?

How will researchers be able to view the finding aid created for my collection? How will researchers access the collections themselves? What are your rules for use of the collections?

How does my collection fit in with others at your institution? Is my collection a suitable addition to the institution's holdings? Does it fill a gap in the collections? What role in the overall collection does the repository see for my materials?

dispersed. Links and references to the collection can be made from alternate repositories that take an interest in your materials. You may request that the repository to which you donate items contact other area and related repositories to tell them about the donation once it is accessioned.

If you are ready to donate materials or to establish a relationship with a repository, call or send a letter of inquiry that describes the artifacts you would like to offer. Approach only one repository at a time. Do not send out mass mailings offering your collection. You may find more than one repository is interested, which could complicate the donation process, as well as cause hard feelings or aggravation for you and those to whom you reach out.

Never send materials through the mail without the repository agreeing to this. Do not deposit your materials on the institution's doorstep expecting that it will take care of it and take it in. (This happens more often than I would like to recount.) Treat your materials as a valuable resource. Respect the repository's procedures for reviewing items, and if your materials are found suitable for their collections, work with staff to make the transfer of your personal papers as smooth as possible for the safety of your information and to preserve your legacy.

Archives should seek materials that fill gaps in their collections. An institution should use a collection-development policy as a guide. In fact, if the repository does not have a collection-development policy, I am suspicious of their professionalism and would not donate my materials to them. When offered a collection that is better suited for another repository, you and the institution are best served when it recommends another place for your donation. Do not be put off if it turns away your collection. A professionally run institution carefully evaluates whether your materials fit within the guidelines it has established for its holdings.

Recognize that it can be difficult for some smaller institutions, for a variety of reasons related to finances and visibility, to turn away a donor who insists that his collection belongs at their repository. Try to locate an appropriate organization to approach to donate your materials. It will benefit both you and the Archives in the long run. Properly placing materials makes it easier for researchers to find what they need, makes a repository's mission stronger and more successful by focusing what they do, and allows them to give your materials the attention that they deserve. Ask an archivist who turns you away to make a suggestion for a more appropriate place for your donation if he does not do this automatically.

It does not benefit the Archives or the historical record for an institution to accept a collection because of competitiveness, desire for monetary gain, or publicity, if the collection clearly falls outside the realm of the institution's focus. This is an ethical issue with which all archivists must struggle. If you have a high-profile collection, do your homework to ensure that your materials will truly strengthen the overall focus of certain organizations' collections. Giving your materials to a high-profile institution just so you can say that your materials are housed there does not benefit your legacy, research, or the historical record. Aim to fit your materials appropriately so they are easy to find and access, and that they relate well to the other collections with which they will be housed.

You should be prepared to ask questions about the place where you are considering donating your materials. Well-known repositories should provide a safe environment for collections, but one should not just assume that an institution is run with high standards. Institutions have highly variable storage conditions, staffing, and procedures for the care of materials. Ensure that the institution to which you propose to donate materials is professionally run. Even organizations run by volunteers have the capability of implementing professional standards. To ensure that your materials will be well cared for, make sure that they have policies in place for their care.

Make sure that the institution has climate control and uses preservation-safe materials for housing items. Many smaller repositories do not have fancy climate-control systems, and sometimes this is all right. In this case, refer to the preservation section of this book and ask about the building environment and shelving. Are materials stored in an interior room? Have temperature and humidity fluctuations been calculated? Are there any plans for climate control in the future? Do they have a disaster plan? Ask about the institution's backlog. It is normal for most institutions to have many groups of materials in line for processing, but you should not have to wait for years for them to make your materials available to researchers. Ask them about when they expect to have the processing and finding aids for your collection complete. Ask what kind of finding aid they might make for your materials and if you can see their research tools for other collections. Do they make unprocessed materials available to researchers? If they do, be aware that the risk of theft or misplacement greatly increases for collections in such circumstances.[65]

Researchers should also be asked to fill out a reference form and follow some basic rules for the use of archival material, including such things as no researchers allowed in the storage area, no book bags in the research room, and the use of only pencils and not pens. Ask exactly how the staff sees your materials fitting in with others in their collection. Do they have other materials similar to yours? Why is your collection of interest to them, and does it fit within their mission and collection-development guidelines?

---

[65] For information about collection security, see Karen E. Brown and Beth Lindblom Patkus, "Collections Security: Planning and Prevention for Libraries and Archives," *Northeast Document Conservation Center Preservation*, www.nedcc.org/resources/leaflets/3Emergency_Management/11CollectionsSecurity.php (July 29, 2011).

Rules for Use of the Collections

You want to ensure that you are giving your materials to a responsible repository. The following is a list of some of the more common rules for use to which archives require their users to adhere. Make sure that your chosen repository has a similar set of rules to confirm their professionalism.

- The repository asks users to complete a reference request to assist with service and to keep track of materials used.
- Repositories do not permit researchers in areas where archives are stored. The archivist will retrieve materials requested by researchers.
- An archivist must be present while a researcher uses archival materials.
- Users must handle items with care. They must use pencil to take notes. They may be required to wear gloves. They will be asked to keep materials flat on the desk.
- Users must leave coats, briefcases, and bags outside the reading room.
- Users must maintain materials in original order.
- Users must abide by copyright laws and seek permission from the repository to publish from original materials under their care.
- Items may not be removed from the archives.

Preparing Your Papers for Transfer

A repository's archivist will fully process any materials that you have, but there are some things that you can do to assist them. It is valuable for the person to whom you transfer your papers to know as much about their context as possible. Use the guidelines throughout this book to organize, preserve, and describe your materials as thoroughly as you can. The following paragraphs give a summary of what you can do to help an archivist better care for your materials.

First, make sure you have the right to donate this material. Are you the legitimate owner of these physical items and the copyright owner? If the materials were not created by you and were not formally given to you in writing, speak to other appropriate family members about their wishes for this material. For example, if the records belonged to your parents, do your siblings have any claim to them? How do they feel about donating them to a repository?

When you have confirmed that you are prepared to transfer materials, write information on a piece of paper that you will put in the front of your collection or hand over separately. If you are not comfortable writing about your materials, record yourself talking about them. If the papers you are donating are not your own, aim to describe as completely as possible the person or people who created the collection. Define your relationship to them. Provide some background information about yourself if the records were created by you. Provide biographical information, if possible, and dates of important events in individuals' lives. Note any important features of the collection. These features may be obvious from the materials themselves. Or, an item in the collection may relate to a topic, but its implications may not be obvious. For example, if your mother has a flyer related to the civil rights movement and marched with Dr. Martin Luther King, tell the archivist. Look through your collection to seek information that might confuse an outsider. Consider the context of items and offer explanations where needed. Label photographs with a pencil or preservation-safe pen and include names, dates, events, and locations.

Try to keep materials with their original organization scheme. Do not try to impose a better organizational system. Instead, focus your efforts on supplying backup information that will assist the archivist with her job. It is likely that anyone researching about some part of your life will want to know more about you than you can conceive at the moment and, as I discussed earlier in this book, your organization is a unique and sometimes telling aspect of your materials.

When preparing your items for transfer, think about your needs. Will you want some kind of access to this material once you do not "own" it? The repository likely will not let you leave the building with materials (nor should they), but they may accommodate you by making copies when you need them. It is sometimes best if you make copies before you give your materials to the repository. Consider if you want to scan your items. Will you be allowed to publish from your materials? Ask what to expect, and do not make assumptions.

Making Your Donation Official

You should not be surprised if the archives to which you are offering your materials would like to see them before any agreement is made about their deposit. Again, this speaks to the idea that archivists want to make sure that your materials are a proper fit for their institution. They also may want to check the condition and organization of your materials to see what kind of work they have in store for them so they can properly plan for a potential new accession.

You should expect some formality in the form of official paperwork when you come to an agreement with an archival repository to donate your materials. A lack of paperwork shows a lack of professionalism. You should never "hand over" your papers to a repository that lacks a donor agreement form. The donor agreement form gives the institution permission to keep your materials as it sees fit, giving it property rights to your collection. This basically means that it will own your materials so it can process them, shelve them, and otherwise incorporate them into its general holdings. The donor agreement form should also ask you to sign over "intellectual property" rights. This gives the archives the right to administer the content of the materials. An institution may own papers, but it may not have the final say in who gets to publish from them or may not even have the right to use the information in the documents to the benefit of the institution. If you do not sign over the

Papers of Robert Kennedy

While presidential papers created after 1978 are subject to the Presidential Records Act, which makes them accessible to the public after a certain number of years, those of John F. Kennedy are not—and those of his brother, Robert Kennedy, remain in his family's control. Housed at the JFK Library in Boston, the records were recently targeted by the media in reports calling for unrestricted access. RFK's papers have been kept under tight seal, which disturbs historians and others who suspect there is a whole lot of great information in there. People want to learn more about the Cuban Missile Crisis, and some suspect there are many more revealing stories in the collection. Rumors fly when records are inaccessible, leaving us with romantic tales of untouched documentary evidence.

intellectual property right, people will have to come to you or your ancestors for permission to use the ideas in your personal papers. In general, this does not work to anyone's benefit. If you trust an institution to care for your items, you should trust them to administer them in total. Most institutions will not accept your records with caveats and will require you to allow them full control so that they may maintain the materials up to professional standards on par with all of the other collections they maintain.

Sometimes donors give papers with stipulations. The one that I have seen most often is when a collection is donated under the condition that it remains sealed until the creator of the collection dies. Sometimes a donor requests that the repository wait a certain number of years after that person's death or until direct descendants have also passed. Donors are sometimes concerned that the information in their papers could be damaging to a reputation or might reveal something that can harm loved ones.[66]

If you are concerned about giving up your materials but recognize their value to a potential larger audience, you may be thinking about donating copies of your personal papers. Archives aim to add original/unique materials into their collections. They rarely accept copies, preferring to hold the original sources that serve as primary substantiation of history. Institutions will sometimes (rarely) make exceptions, but it does not hurt to ask about their policy on this matter. Express your concerns and let them alleviate them.

These days, organizations are delving more and more into digital projects. These projects usually involve the holdings residing at cultural institutions, but if your materials are unique, you do not want to part with them just yet, and you think your community may benefit from a digitizing project, you can offer scanned copies of what you have in lieu of originals. It does not hurt to bring up the idea with your local archivist, but do not get your hopes up. Digital projects are expensive and time-consuming and just may not fit in with your target repository's agenda.

---

[66] For more on the Robert Kennedy papers described in the text box on the previous page, see Joan Venocchi's "Release RFK's Records," *Boston Globe,* Jan. 30, 2011, www.boston.com/bostonglobe/editorial_opinion/oped/articles/2011/01/30/release_rfks_records (July 29, 2011).

Collections with Monetary Value

Some of your materials may have more than informational value. Many historic items have monetary value. In the United States, archivists and curators are prohibited from providing you with monetary appraisals of your items.[67] In fact, in the United States, few would have the expertise to know the fair market value of manuscripts.[68] Libraries, Archives, and museums cannot perform a monetary appraisal because the Internal Revenue Service sees it as a conflict of interest, believing it may be desirable to convince a potential donor to make a gift in exchange for a high appraisal of the donated item that will be claimed on tax forms. Donors wanting an appraisal must themselves locate and pay a professional appraiser.[69]

Like artwork and other unique items, documents are worth what someone is willing to pay for them. While certain subjects or authors of documents obviously command buyers, others may not be so apparent. The signatures of famous figures alone are prized by collectors willing to pay. Items of noteworthy subjects with signatures are even more highly prized by collectors. If you have materials written by people of note in your possession, consider having a monetary appraisal performed by a reputable dealer to gain a better understanding of your assets.

The value of most family papers may be less obvious to the casual observer. For example, an individual's account of a certain event may fill a niche for a collector. Consider, for one, letters and photos of enlisted Civil War soldiers that are often highly prized. It is a good idea to think about your personal papers for monetary worth so they can be appropriately insured if necessary and so that you can get a tax writeoff if you do eventually donate materials to a repository. Making a list of items is useful for keeping track of your possessions and will help highlight items of monetary value for the future.

Museums, libraries, and Archives sometimes end up competing for valuable documents against collectors. Collectors may value items because of a

---

[67] See "IRS Publication 561" regarding donations of property; specifically, the section on "Qualified Appraisal: Excluded Individuals," www.irs.gov/publications/p561/ar02.html#d0e1653 (July 29, 2011).

[68] In other countries, it is exactly opposite of what one finds in the United States. and archivists perform monetary appraisal as a regular part of their jobs. Canada, for one, is different from the United States. See David Walden's "Stretching the Dollar: Monetary Appraisal of Manuscripts," *Archivaria, Number 11 (Winter 1980-81)*, bit.ly/coKLV3 (July 29, 2011).

[69] To find a reputable appraiser, contact The Appraisers Association of America (www.appraisersassoc.org) or the American Society of Appraisers (www.appraisers.org/ASAHome.aspx).

personal interest in a particular subject or may just wish to collect something of value. While there is nothing wrong with collecting (it can be a fun and exciting hobby), individuals wishing to let go of historical items should consider donating them to an institution before selling them to an individual buyer. Such records could be important pieces of the historical record, filling a gap in the history that cultural heritage institutions try hard to preserve. The individual's role as a cultural heritage collaborator is an important one, and everyone should recognize that they can play a strong part in ensuring the transfer of information to future generations through the memory institutions that are sworn to safeguard it.

Many archives do not purchase collections because they do not have the funding for this. In cases where archives do purchase, they actively seek materials that will enhance or fill gaps in their collections. However, these institutions use their money to purchase high-profile collections. Though an institution may appreciate and evaluate your personal papers as a donation, unless you have something very unique that relates to a subject with a high profile, an Archives will likely not seek to purchase your materials. Your good deed can be rewarded, at least in part, through tax deductions. Consult a lawyer for more information about this.

Consider the value of your materials to future generations. They may come looking for pieces of their history that have been torn apart by antique dealers who sell items individually as collectibles or curiosities. I enjoy browsing and sometimes purchasing ephemera and other family materials I find in antique shops, but I am often heartbroken at the nameless people who stare back at me in photos. Romantic sentiments that I find in personal letters may once have had meaning to a sender and recipient, but they are often sold off in bundles by later generations who do not know what to do with them. History is lost when items are separated from others, stripping them of context and provenance. An archives repository can help you ensure that your family history will be preserved and waiting for future generations. The value of finding old family letters for family members themselves and communities interested in them can be immeasurable, while individual items generally are sold in the market for a few dollars. I have found all kinds of papers with historical value in antique shops. Even public government records that are legally owned by the municipalities that created them can be readily found in shops. Everything has some monetary value, but is it really worth a few bucks to sell off your heritage and memories of your past? Preserve your heritage, and that of your family and your community, for posterity.

Family Heritage for Sale

I attended an estate sale with my young daughter. We arrived by mid-morning on the second day of the event. The sale had been advertised by a local high-end secondhand store that I like to frequent. Cars lined the block with tape and cones, helping to guide us to proper places to park. My daughter and I exited the car and held hands, walking with other curious people toward the event while weaving our way through others returning to their cars. The chandeliers, tools, and glassware that were advertised on the first day were gone by the time we arrived. Some costume jewelry twinkled in glass cases in the sun. While my daughter quickly locked on to a knickknack owl on a table in the garage, I located a box of documents in the corner of the basement. I poked through it to find religious certificates and memorabilia, and while I usually take pleasure in poking through archives, I felt strangely uncomfortable with this box.

My daughter articulated what I was feeling as we climbed the basement steps to return to the car. She said, "Mommy, what happened here?"

Trying to explain estate sales to a seven-year-old is no easy task. I told her that the people who lived in this house no longer wanted these things. I told her that perhaps they were moving to a smaller home or maybe there was just no one who needed these things anymore.

Although I spend most of my time trying to put together the stories of communities and lives, I felt like the stories were being shattered in this home. What did the objects mean to the people who owned them? Were all of the items appropriate for this sales event? How would these people be remembered? How did these people or those who cared for them decide what to keep and what to give away?

I remember when my grandmother passed away when I was a teenager. My father flew down to her house and took care of her estate, quickly going through her artifacts, deciding what to keep and what to discard. For all I knew, he based decisions on personal sentiment at a very emotional time. That is not how any child should have to deal with family memories—the accumulations and documentation of a long life quickly considered rather than contentedly pondered and secured.

Few people think about what parts of their life should be recorded for posterity. Few consider their life in the context of their community or a larger culture that needs the stories of individuals to tell a fuller tale of humanity. "Other people's useless stuff" makes me wonder: What "other people"? Who makes decisions about what is important to a life? Although people may take old objects and treasure them anew, an object can embody many life stories. What are the best ways for us to share the history of an object with our loved ones? Perhaps we might even want to share some histories with communities or other people who value our material after we no longer want or need it?

—*From the ArchivesInfo blog (September 10, 2010) "Deconstructing a Life"*

My Memories, Your Memories

In planning for the future, I recognize that my memories are just one thread of narrative in a larger human story. I envision my personal papers lined up neatly in archival boxes alongside yours, waiting for our descendants and for future generations of historians to try to make sense of our times. While examining our materials, they will consider a larger framework of history and their own cultural landscape. They will possess hindsight about the way civilization progressed from our point forward to make sense of their own place in the world.

In a passage from one of my favorite books, *A Place to Remember*, respected public historian Robert Archibald states:

> …But the past itself does not stay around awaiting our interpretations. What we can know of the past is only what is left. Some of it is left to us intentionally by humans who wished us to remember them in certain ways, and more of it survives accidentally. These things are the only evidence we possess of times before our own. Yet, what remains is a minuscule portion of the past; and, because so much of it survives serendipitously, we cannot presume it to be either a representative or comprehensive sample. Despite the paucity of evidence, we persist in assuming that the past is knowable and comprehensible…[70]

We have a role in the future. What we create today can be what is left for interpretation if we take steps to safeguard and explain it. Our personal papers are part of the evidence about which Archibald speaks. My memories separate from yours are not "representative or comprehensive," but together among other community papers, our memories can be both. When planning for the future, help leave behind tangible knowledge that will equip humanity to build a better society. "Creating and Maintaining Family Papers, Photographs, and Memorabilia" is not just a nice idea: It is a vital part of what keeps civilization moving ahead. Give our descendants the memories of all of our most informative successes, mistakes, and stories so that they may learn from them and grow.

---

[70] Robert Archibald, *A Place to Remember: Using History to Build Community* (MD: AltaMira Press, 1999), 212–213.

Specialized Archives with Personal Papers

Many research institutions maintain specialized archives that document a particular area of interest. Below is a smattering of varied collections in the United States.

American Jewish Archives (Hebrew Union College, Jewish Institute of Religion)— The Archives is committed to preserving a documentary heritage of the religious, organizational, economic, cultural, personal, social, and family life of American Jewry. americanjewisharchives.org

Baltimore Museum of Industry—The archives at the Baltimore Museum of Industry house many wonderful documents that allow us to tell the story of local companies. www.thebmi.org/page/archives

The Human Sexuality Collection (Cornell University)—One of the first of its kind in the United States, this collection "seeks to preserve and make accessible primary sources that document historical shifts in the social construction of sexuality." rmc.library.cornell.edu/HSC

Immigration History Research Center (University of Minnesota)—The center "promotes research on international migration with a special emphasis on immigrant and refugee life" in the United States. www.ihrc.umn.edu

The John Hope Franklin Research Center for African and African American History and Culture (Duke University)—This repository "seeks to collect, preserve, and promote the use of library materials bearing on the history of Africa and people of African descent." library.duke.edu/specialcollections/franklin

The Niels Bohr Library & Archives for the American Institute of Physics— "The Niels Bohr Library & Archives has an outstanding collection of books and print materials in the history of modern physics. [They] are perhaps even better known as an archives that includes major photo, biographical, and institutional history collections; historical records of AIP and its Member Societies; and select collections of the papers of leading physicists." www.aip.org/history/nbl/collections.html

Schlesinger Library on the History of Women in America (Harvard University)—The library "exists to document women's lives and endeavors. Its wealth of resources reveals the wide range of women's activities at home in the United States and abroad from the early nineteenth century to the present day." www.radcliffe.edu/schlesinger_library.aspx

Mental and Writing Exercises for Planning for the Future

1. Make plans to sit down with a family member to review a family album, share heirloom stories (like my mother did with her jewelry box), or leaf through interesting family papers. If you have young children or grandchildren, make discussing family stories a regular part of your lives.

2. Make separate plans to discuss the future of your papers with a responsible adult. Put in writing (preferably in an official document such as a will) what you wish to have done with your papers after your death.

3. Make plans for your digital future. Give an appropriate family member access to your accounts. Explore "digital asset" companies (as discussed in the previous chapter) that can help you with this.

4. Make a list of institutions that may take an interest in your records. Consider what unique content your materials possess that would make it desirable to specific repositories.

5. If your records have value to a larger community outside of your family and you wish to donate them to a repository, call or write to an institution that seems like a good fit. Try to contact the institution's archivist directly. Ask about its collection development policy. Ask to be referred elsewhere if the repository is not interested in your materials.

6. If you have not created a finding aid for your materials, record basic information about your collection, including: name of person(s) who created the records, his or her relationship to you, and biographical information such as birth dates and dates of other important life events. Note important features of the collection.

Collections Mentioned in this Book

Page 22

Coca-Cola Archives

- Fifty years of Coca-Cola television advertisements via Library of Congress
  memory.loc.gov/ammem/ccmphtml/colahome.html
- The Coca-Cola Company Heritage
  www.thecoca-colacompany.com/heritage/ourheritage.html

Disney Archives

- Blowing the Pixie Dust off Disney's Archives
  www.nytimes.com/2009/09/09/movies/09archive.html

Hershey Archives

- Hershey Community Archives
  www.hersheyarchives.org

Timex Museum

- www.timexpo.com/?timexBrand=core

Page 39

The Asphalt Museum

- http://ecs.csus.edu/~gordonvs/asphalt/asphalt.html

Kimchi Museum

- www.lifeinkorea.com/Travel2/seoul/315

Museum of Bad Art (MOBA)

- www.museumofbadart.org

Museum of Toilets

- www.sulabhtoiletmuseum.org

Pages 41–42

Uncovering New Chicago Archives Project

- uncap.lib.uchicago.edu

Page 43

Museum of Fine Arts

- www.mfa.org/collections

Elenita Chickering Collection
- Gardner Museum, Gardner, Massachusetts
  www.thegardnermuseum.com

Page 169-170
My Coney Island Memories
- www.myconeyislandmemories.com

Page 174
American Folklife Center at the Library of Congress
- www.loc.gov/folklife/

Page 193
Salman Rushdie Archives
- Emory University
  www.emory.edu/home/academics/libraries/salman-rushdie.html

Page 198
SepiaTown
- Historical images from around the globe
  www.sepiatown.com

Page 199
Flickr Commons
- www.flickr.com/commons

Page 210
Rebecca West Papers
- Department of Special Collections and University Archives, University of Tulsa
  www.lib.utulsa.edu/speccoll/collections/westrebecca/index.htm
- Beinecke Rare Book and Manuscript Library
  hdl.handle.net/10079/fa/beinecke.westart

Page 217
Robert Kennedy Papers
- www.jfklibrary.org/JFK/The-Kennedy-Family/Robert-F-Kennedy.aspx

Glossary of Selected Professional Archives and Cultural Heritage Terminology

Access points—Informational tools that provide alternate ways to retrieve information from a collection. Access points are created by an archivist by physically arranging materials alphabetically, numerically, or chronologically. More specific entries into the collection are created through intellectual tools (finding aids) that focus on information the archivist chooses to highlight, such as notable persons or events.

Active records—Records that are regularly used in the course of an institution's or individual's regular activities. Such records can be used daily, weekly, or monthly and should be maintained in offices where they can be readily accessed and not within archival repositories. Some active records may be deemed important for posterity (as archives) and should be moved to an Archives once they are no longer regularly needed.

Appraisal—The process of determining the permanent value of records and thus where they end up at the end of their active lives. The determination of value is based on the evidence and information the records provide, their arrangement and condition, intrinsic worth, and relationship to other records. The archival concept of appraisal is distinct from those in other fields that use the word to primarily refer to an item's monetary worth.

Archival survey—A formal project conducted to determine the scope of materials in an institution or community.

Archives—
1. Materials relating to the history of an institution that are kept for permanent preservation because of their evidential or informational value (e.g., documents, photographs, books, maps, blueprints). "Archives" is sometimes used as an umbrella term that encompasses both institutional records and "personal papers" or "manuscripts."
2. The location at which archival materials are maintained.

3. The organization that cares for archival materials (i.e., the people, archivist, manuscript curator).

Archivist—A person, usually with specialized training, who cares for archival materials. Archivists generally have advanced degrees in history or library science, with specific study in the area of archives management. Some archivists also possess certification in the field. Archivists can work at any institution that wants to maintain its records but are most often employed by cultural heritage institutions, universities, or large corporations.

Arrangement—The organization of archival material following a five-level standard hierarchy that includes repository, fonds, series, subseries, and items.

Artifact—An object created by a human, usually for a practical purpose. In the field of cultural heritage, refers to materials that are retained for their historical value. The term generally refers to nonarchival items, but in the broadest sense of the word, archives are included among artifacts.

Artificial arrangement—An organizational scheme applied to a record collection by an archivist and not by the collection's original creator.

Blog—A website that invites interaction on which one makes regular entries related to newsworthy events or individual experiences. It often serves as a type of journal and can be considered a modern diary.

Born digital—Materials that originated in electronic form, as opposed to things that were changed to this form. Used to describe records that were created on a computer, as opposed to paper files that were scanned or otherwise converted to a digital format.

Buffered paper—Paper washed in the manufacturing process with an alkaline chemical agent such as calcium carbonate. Used in the storage of archives to help neutralize acid contaminants.

Citizen archivist—A controversial, newly coined term adapted by the Archivist of the United States to describe nonprofessionals who maintain personal papers and/or have an interest in promoting the care and security of archival records.

Collection—The contents of an Archives or a specific large group of materials within that Archives.

Collection development policy—The document that defines what an institution collects and what it does not. It sets a direction for the collecting focus of the organization by expanding on the mission statement.

Community—A formal or informal group with a common history or culture. The community can be based around a geographic area, trait, or topic of interest. Communities come in the form of families, ethnic groups, civic organizations, governments, informal and formal social groups, educational institutions, colleagues, causes, and geographical locations/neighborhoods.

Community documentation—
1. Materials collected that help tell a story about a community.
2. The act of gathering records and artifacts that provide diverse information about a community in an attempt to provide a "complete" perspective of that community. This act of gathering records is better known as a "community documentation project."

Crowdsourcing—Inviting a community to help perform tasks and solve problems traditionally addressed by employees or specialists in a certain area. In cultural heritage fields, patrons are asked to help with activities such as assigning metadata or designing exhibits.

Cultural heritage—Tangible items that are considered worthy of preservation for the future due to their reflection of a society's identity. It also encompasses intangible values and customs that are passed from one generation to another.

Cultural heritage institution—An institution that stores materials that represent a society's intellectual and artistic essence and supports the continuance of that society's traditions and memory.

Cultural heritage partner—A person interested in sustaining cultural heritage or one who possesses tangible or intangible cultural heritage items and/or rituals.

Descriptive inventory—A basic tool created by archivists to describe and facilitate access to a collection. A descriptive inventory (i.e., collection guide or manuscript inventory) defines the scope of a collection and its details. Includes scope and content, arrangement, biographical notes, and other descriptive elements, in addition to a list of series to provide a strong overview of the collection.

Diary—A record of concurrent events, often in handwritten form. A diary can be quite varied, ranging from long entries about in-depth experiences and feelings to short entries related to finances or the weather. In the past, diaries were considered private recordings of a person's life. Today, they are becoming more of a public entity in the form of a blog.

Documentary record—The surviving written or otherwise recorded information that provides evidence or information about a society and its activities in a certain time and place.

Donor agreement forms—Documents used to legally transfer material to a collecting repository and to reach out to potential record creators to explain the importance of preserving archives in their care.

Ephemera—Items that are created for a specific event or activity, are often mass-produced, and are not intended to survive indefinitely (e.g., a handbill, newspaper, or menu).

Evidential value—In archival "appraisal," the worth of a record based on its reflection of the organization and the function of the institution or body that created it. Records possessing evidential value provide authentic and adequate evidence of an organization's activities.

Facebook—A popular social networking website that allows registered users to share information. Individual users generally share information about themselves, making it a valuable documentation site.

Finding aids—Indices to a collection that help establish intellectual control over the archives. Basic finding aids include descriptive inventories, guides, accession registers, card catalogues, shelf lists, and automated databases.

Historical value—The worth of material based on its importance to the cultural heritage.

Historical record—The recorded information used to evaluate and interpret the past.

Information resource—A document or other man-made item that communicates knowledge about an event, place, living being, or object, or that conveys ideas related to any subject.

Informational value—In archival appraisal, the worth of a record based on the information it contains.

Institutional archives—The records collected to document the history of an institution such as a government body, business, or nonprofit organization.

Intellectual control—The management of archives through descriptive documents resulting from the process of arrangement and description.

Interleaving paper—Paper (often buffered) placed between documents to help prevent damage caused by friction or acid migration.

Intrinsic value—The worth of material based on monetary or sentimental value.

Level of arrangement—Hierarchical divisions of organization used to describe archival collections. These levels include collection, repository, record group, fonds, subgroups, series, subseries, files, and items.

Level of description—The amount of detail provided to describe archival material in a finding aid.

Lifestream—A chronological stream of documents that functions as a diary of your electronic life.

Magnetic album—An album with pages that have a sticky back on which one can tack photographs. The pages are usually covered by plastic sheets. These pages were popular in the 1970s and 1980s and are not safe for archival materials.

Manuscript inventory—See *descriptive inventory*.

Material culture—Any physical item created by a person or a society that possesses "historical value."

Memorabilia—A memento or keepsake that reminds one of a past event.

Memory institution—Institutions such as Archives, museums, and libraries that serve to preserve and keep cultural heritage in the form of collections and thus seek to pass down as much human knowledge developed through time as possible.

Metadata—Structured information that identifies, describes, and classifies the features of artifacts, such as its creator, subject, and format. Used to "tag" materials so that they can later be easily located and used.

Microclimate—The climate of a small, specific place within an area as contrasted with the climate of the entire area. In archives management, a box used for storing materials has the effect of changing the environmental conditions by providing separation from the larger surroundings.

Mission statement—A declaration that defines the purpose of an institution or program.

Natural collection—A collection of materials arranged on the principles of "Provenance" and "Sanctity of Original Order."

Off gas—Chemicals emitted from materials that can potentially harm documents and artifacts.

Oxidation—A loss of electrons or an increase in oxidation state by a molecule, atom, or ion due to an oxidation agent such as oxygen in the air, ozone, or pollutants such as nitrogen oxide. In some cases, light (particularly UV light) acts as a catalyst in activating these oxidants. In the preservation of archival material, oxidation leads to the deterioration of material.

PDF—Portable document format. A file format that is highly portable across computer platforms. It is the recognized standard for the preservation of documents with long-term significance. It uses a .pdf file extension.

Personal papers—Materials relating to an individual that are often housed in a "Special Collections" or are kept as part of a family collection.

Physical control—The management of archives through their tangible organization resulting from "processing" and taking into account the archival principle of the five levels of arrangement.

Preservation copy—A duplicate of a record that is often created in an alternative format to the original to help ensure the long-term retention of the information found within that original record.

Preservation survey—A formal project that assesses the state of materials within a collection by evaluating the materials' housing environment, the storage materials in which the archives are kept, and the condition of the materials themselves.

Primary source—Unique, recorded information that was created contemporaneously with the time it illustrates, by a person who participated in the recorded events. Primary sources include, but are not limited to, photographs, diaries, and ledgers. They are distinguished from secondary sources.

Processing—The act of organizing, describing, and preserving archival material in a repository to ensure its safety and to make it available for access.

Provenance—
1. The origin of a collection; documents the life of the collection (e.g., donor, previous owners of the collection).
2. The archival strategy of not intermingling records from different creators or donors. The "creator" is an organization or individual who wrote, accumulated, and/or maintained and used the records in the conduct of their business or personal life.

Public records—Local, state, or federal government–created documents that serve a public purpose and are subject to laws related to their maintenance and distribution.

Record group—A large grouping of materials within a collection (e.g., the records created by a department within a municipality may be considered a record group).

Record life cycle—Refers to the original purpose for which a record is created and its subsequent uses. A record is most actively used soon after its creation. With the passage of time, the primary purpose for which a document is created elapses or users need to access the document less frequently. The phases of the record life cycle include: Creation, Use, Maintenance (i.e., storage, retrieval, and protection), Disposition (i.e., transfer to a less expensive, temporary storage area), Destruction, and Transfer (to archives).

Records—Documents in any form containing information created by an organization during the course of the institution's daily activities.

Records management—The function that controls the creation, maintenance, and disposition of information created by an institution. Records management involves controlling the creation of forms and deciding what types of records need to be generated by departments. The records management function also controls the flow of paper through the creation of an inventory and schedules that detail how long paper should be kept and when it should be moved to alternate storage.

Relative humidity—The ratio of the amount of water in the air at a given temperature to the maximum amount of water it has the potential to hold at that given temperature.

Scope and content—The description of a collection or its parts.

Secondary sources—Nonoriginal and mass-produced materials such as photocopies and published items, including news clippings, books, and journal articles. These materials are generally separated from archival resources for preservation purposes, to distinguish them from primary resources, and to reduce supply costs. These materials are not generally created contemporaneously with the events they describe as the events occur.

Series—Records, generally with the same provenance, that have a similar theme, result from the same activity, or have similar formats. Within the five levels of arrangement, the level that falls below the fonds. The series records are generally the most commonly described groups of records within archival finding aids—primarily, the descriptive inventory.

Social media—Tools on the Internet for communication between multiple individuals that results in the creation of online, generally permanent, information content. Social media includes blogs, social networks such as Facebook and LinkedIn, video sharing such as YouTube, photo sharing such as Flickr, and more.

Special collections—Groups of personal papers, such as those generally found in an historical society, usually relating to an individual or family.

Twitter—A social networking site that allows users to make short posts (called tweets) of up to 140 characters that are seen by the user's followers. The Library of Congress began "archiving" tweets in 2010, recognizing them as a valuable form of communication and documentation.

Vital records—Those records essential to the continued functioning of an organization or of prime importance to an individual's life. Vital records include such materials as birth, death, and marriage records; incorporation papers; charters; and deeds.

Weeding—The process of removing unwanted materials from a collection.

Bibliography

Albright, Gary. "Storage Enclosures for Photographic Materials." *NEDCC Technical Preservation Leaflet 4.11.* 2007. www.nedcc.org/resources/leaflets/4Storage_and_Handling/11StorageEnclosures.php (July 31, 2011).

The American Institute for Conservation of Historic and Artistic Works (AIC). "Ten Tips for the Homeowner." www.conservation-us.org/index.cfm?fuseaction=Page.viewPage&pageId=597 (July 31, 2011).

Association for Information and Image Management (AIIM). "PDF/A: The Development of a Digital Preservation Standard." August 2005. www.aiim.org/documents/standards/PDF-A/PDFA69thSAA805.pdf (July 31, 2011).

———. "Image File Format Standards: TIFF, JPEG, and PDF. Different Formats for Different Jobs." January/February 2006. www.aiim.org/Infonomics/ArticleView.aspx?id=31178 (July 31, 2011).

Archibald, Robert. *A Place to Remember: Using History to Build Community.* Walnut Creek, CA: AltaMira Press, 1999.

Archivist of the United States. "Cultivating Citizen Archivists." April 12, 2010. blogs.archives.gov/aotus/?p=144 (July 31, 2011).

ASTM. "Paper Aging." cool.conservation-us.org/coolaic/sg/bpg/annual/v19/bp19-01.html

Boles, Frank. "Disrespecting Original Order." *American Archivist* 45, no. 1 (Winter 1982): 26–32.

Brown, Karen, and Beth Lindblom Patkus. "Collections Security: Planning and Prevention for Libraries and Archives." *Northeast Document Conservation Center Preservation Leaflet 3.11.* 2007. www.nedcc.org/resources/leaflets/3Emergency_Management/11CollectionsSecurity.php (July 31, 2011).

Buchanan, Sally. "Emergency Salvage of Wet Books and Records." *Northeast Document Conservation Center Preservation Leaflet 3.6.* 2007.

www.nedcc.org/resources/leaflets/3Emergency_Management/06SalvageW
etBooks.php (July 31, 2011).

Burge, Daniel M. "Just What Is the Photographic Activity Test?" *Picture
Framing Magazine,* February1996.
www.pictureframingmagazine.com/pdfs/conservpres/Feb96_photoactivity
.pdf (July 31, 2011).

The Center for the Study of History and Memory at Indiana University,
Bloomington. "Oral History Techniques: How to Organize and Conduct
Oral History Interviews." www.indiana.edu/~cshm/techniques.html (July
31, 2011).

Cohen, Patricia. "Fending Off Digital Decay Bit by Bit." *New York Times* (New
York, NY), March 15, 2010.
www.nytimes.com/2010/03/16/books/16archive.html?pagewanted=all
(July 31, 2011).

Cox, Richard J. "Digital Curation and the Citizen Archivist." d-
scholarship.pitt.edu/2692/1/CoxOfficialSubmissionRevision.pdf (July 31,
2011).

Cunningham, Sally Jo, Masood Masoodian, and Anne Adams. "Privacy Issues for
Online Personal Photograph Collection." *Journal of Theoretical and
Applied Electronic Commerce Research* 5, no. 2 (August 2010): 26–40.

Dahlø, Rolf. "The Rationale of Permanent Paper." 64th IFLA General Conference,
16–21 August 1998, cool.conservation-us.org/byauth/dahlo/rationale.html
(July 31, 2011).

Drewes, Jeanne. *"Mold,* Pests, and Dust*:* Preservation Policies and Management."
International Preservation News, 42 (October 2007): 40–42.
archive.ifla.org/VI/4/news/ipnn42.pdf (July 31, 2011).

Dupleix, Jill, and Terry Durack. "Write Your Own Food Biography: My Life in
Ten Dishes." July 2010. www.theage.com.au/entertainment/blogs/table-
talk/write-your-own-food-biography-my-life-in-10-dishes/20100729-
10xrd.html (July 31, 2011).

Freeman, Eric, and David Gelernter. "Lifestreams: Organizing Your Electronic
Life." cs-www.cs.yale.edu/homes/freeman/lifestreams.html (July 31,
2011).

FSO Technologies, Inc. "Recordkeeping Guide: How Long Should You Retain Your Records?" (July 31, 2011).

Fulton, Wayne. "A Few Scanning Tips." www.scantips.com (July 31, 2011).

Georgia State Archives. "Essential Records for Families: What You Need to Know Before You Evacuate." sos.georgia.gov/archives/how_may_we_help_you/emergency_advice/evacuation_records.pdf (July 31, 2011).

Goodwin, Doris Kearns. *Wait Till Next Year: A Memoir*. New York, New York: Touchstone, 1997.

Herring Wilson, Emily, ed. *Two Gardeners: Katharine S. White and Elizabeth Lawrence—A Friendship in Letters*. Boston: Beacon Press, 2002.

Internal Revenue Service. "IRS Publication 552: Record Keeping for Individuals." www.irs.gov/pub/irs-pdf/p552.pdf (July 31, 2011).

Jones, William. "Keeping Found Things Found: The Study and Practice of Personal Information Management." 2008. searchdatamanagement.techtarget.com/feature/Personal-information-management-History-and-details (July 31, 2011).

Kolar, Jana, Matija Strlic, and John B.G.A. Havermans, eds. *Proceedings of the International Conference Durability of Paper and Writing*. Ljubljana, Slovenia: National and University Library, 2004.

Library of Congress. "Personal Archiving: Preserving Your Digital Memories." www.digitalpreservation.gov/you/index.html (July 31, 2011).

Marshall, Catherine C. "Rethinking Personal Digital Archiving Part I: Four Challenges from the Field." *D-Lib Magazine* 14, no. 3/4 (March/April 2008). (July 31, 2011).

———. "Rethinking Personal Digital Archiving Part II: Implications for Services, Applications, and Institutions." *D-Lib Magazine* 14, no. 3/4 (March/April 2008). (July 31, 2011).

The National Disaster Education Coalition. "Family Disaster Plan." www.disastercenter.com/guide/family.htm (July 31, 2011).

National Park Service. "Museum Handbook." www.nps.gov/history/museum/publications/MHI/mushbkI.html (July 31, 2011).

New York State Archives. "Appraisal of Historical Records." www.archives.nysed.gov/a/records/mr_pub50_introduction.shtml (July 31, 2011).

Norris, Linda. "How Do You Put People in the Picture of Local History? 2 Smart Ideas." *The Uncataloged Museum*, November 2010. uncatalogedmuseum.blogspot.com/2010/11/how-do-you-put-people-in-picture-of.html (July 31, 2011).

Ogden, Sherelyn. "Storage Furniture: A Brief Review of Current Options." *NEDCC Preservation Leaflet*. 2007.

Patkus, Beth Linblom. "Emergency Salvage of Moldy Books and Paper." *NEDCC Preservation Leaflet.* www.nedcc.org/resources/leaflets/3Emergency_Management/08SalvageMoldyBooks.php (July 31, 2011).

Peters, Dale. "Climates and Microclimates: A New Attitude to the Storage of Archival Material." *AMLIB Newsletter* (Association of Archivists and Manuscript Librarians) 60 (May 1996): 8–12. cool.conservation-us.org/byauth/peters/peters1.html (July 31, 2011).

Peterson, Kristen A. and Thomas Murphy. *Waltham Rediscovered: An Ethnic History of Massachusetts.*Portsmouth, NH: Peter E. Randall Publisher, 1988.

Porck, Henk J., and Rene Teygler. *Preservation Science Survey: An Overview of Recent Development in Research on the Conservation of Selected Analog Library and Archival Materials.* Council on Library and Information Resources: December 2000.

Ritzenthaler, Mary Lynn. *Preserving Archives and Manuscripts (2nd ed.).* Chicago: Society of American Archivists, 2010.

Ritzenthaler, Mary Lynn, Gerald J. Munoff, and Margery S. Long. *Archives and Manuscripts: Administration of Photographic Collections.* Chicago: Society of American Archivists, 1984.

Shapiro, Kortney. "Our Inheritance Is the Survivors' Legacy." *The Canadian Jewish News,* Feb. 10, 2011.

Society of American Archivists. "A Guide to Donating Your Personal or Family Papers to a Repository." www.archivists.org/publications/donating-familyrecs.asp (July 31, 2011).

Strlic, Matija. "Why Does Paper Degrade?" *Papylum Project Aims.* www.science4heritage.org/papylum/aims2.htm (July 31, 2011).

Swallow, Erica. "7 Ways to Handle Digital Life After Death." *Mashable.* Oct. 11, 2010. mashable.com/2010/10/11/social-media-after-death (July 31, 2011).

Truesdell, Barbara. "Oral History Techniques: How to Organize and Conduct Oral History Interviews." *Center for the Study of History and Memory, Indiana University, Bloomington.* www.indiana.edu/~cshm/techniques.html (July 31, 2011).

Ulrich, Laurel Thatcher. *A Midwife's Tale: The Life of Martha Ballard Based on Her Diary, 1785–1812.* New York: Alfred A. Knopf, Inc., 1990.

UNESCO. "Impact of Environmental Pollution on the Preservation of Archives and Records: A RAMP Study." 1988. www.unesco.org/webworld/ramp/html/r8818e/r8818e00.htm (July 31, 2011).

Van Bogart, John. "Magnetic Tape Storage and Handling: A Guide for Libraries and Archives." *National Media Laboratory.* June 1995. www.clir.org/pubs/reports/pub54/1introduction.html (July 31, 2011).

Venocchi, Joan. "Release RFK's Records." *Boston Globe,* Jan. 30, 2011. www.boston.com/bostonglobe/editorial_opinion/oped/articles/2011/01/30/release_rfks_records (July 31, 2011).

West, Sue. "The Tales and the Evidence." *Organizing for the Next Chapter of Your Life.* November 2009. organizenh.com/wordpress/2009/11/the-tales-and-the-evidence (July 31, 2011).

Whitney, Diana. "Am I Jewish?," *Washington Post,* Aug. 30, 2010. newsweek.washingtonpost.com/onfaith/guestvoices/2010/08/am_i_jewish.html (July 31, 2011).

Index

The Unofficial Family Archivist

13328569R00142

Made in the USA
Lexington, KY
25 January 2012